Motorbooks International

FARM TRACTOR COLOR HISTORY

FARMALL
TRACTORS

Text by Robert N. Pripps
Photography by Andrew Morland

To Seth and Tyler Pripps, my nine-year-old grandsons (cousins)—good little guys who already appreciate old tractors

First published in 1993 by Motorbooks International Publishers & Wholesalers, PO Box 2, 729 Prospect Avenue, Osceola, WI 54020 USA

Motorbooks International books are also available at discounts in bulk quantity for industrial or sales-promotional use. For details write to Special Sales Manager at the Publisher's address

Library of Congress Cataloging-in-Publication Data
Pripps, Robert N.
    Farmall tractors / Robert N. Pripps, Andrew Morland.
      p.   cm. —(Motorbooks International farm tractor color history)
    Includes index.
    ISBN 0-87938-763-7
    1. IHC tractors—History.
2. International Harvester Company.
I. Morland, Andrew.   II. Title.
III. Series.
TL233.5.P74   1993
629.225—dc20   93-13162

Printed and bound in Hong Kong

On the front cover: A 1956 Farmall 300, serial number 14787, owned and restored by Austin Hurst. The tractor was bought new by Hurst's father, who sold it in 1969; Hurst later found and repurchased the family heirloom. *Andrew Morland*

On the back cover: Mary Lou and John Poch's Farmall F-12, Serial Number FS74322. John restored the F-12 about five years ago. The F-12 was rated for one 14in plow, and could plow about four acres in a 10hr day on 5gal of gasoline. While rubber tires were optional on the F-12 from the beginning, the Poch collection is entirely on steel.

On the frontispiece: Lady, a registered Guernsey, appears to be appreciating the classic lines of the Farmall Super H. Lady is one of several Guernseys on the Langy farm near Lena, Illinois.

On the title page: White grilles were added to the color scheme in late 1956. Shown here is Jim Polacek's Farmall 200.

Contents

Acknowledgments

My thanks to:

Roger Grozinger of Rusch Equipment Company, Freeport, Illinois, who supplied serial number details and other information about Farmalls. Rusch Equipment is a Case-International dealer.

Austin G. Hurst of Lafayette, California, a private-practice psychiatrist, farm toy collector, and Farmall enthusiast, for technical help and advice with the manuscript for this book.

Andrew Morland, photographer, and Michael Dregni, editor in chief, Motorbooks International Publishing. Without their applied expertise, this book would not have been produced.
Robert N. Pripps

Preface

"Loyalty" is a word not so much in vogue today as it was before the second half of the twentieth century. Loyalties to one's faith, country, flag, political party, and mate were then taken for granted. Today, such fidelity to persons, places, or things is derogatorily referred to as "blind allegiance." Thus, it puzzles some of the younger set when their elders retain brand loyalty for cars, trucks, and tractors.

This devotion is particularly true for tractors, and those who used Farmalls were among the most fanatical. The reasons for this fierce allegiance are many and may be hard to understand if you haven't been there. In the following pages, we will focus on both the times that spawned the Farmall and the tractor's attributes. We may not be able to make a fan out of you, if you're not already one, but we can, perhaps, shed some light on why Farmall fans are so loyal to the mighty Farmall.

The Farmall H was equipped with a 152ci engine, with a rated operating speed of 1650rpm. A five-speed transmission was standard. In Nebraska Test Number 333, the H (with gasoline fuel) developed 24.3 belt and 19.8 drawbar horsepower. While most Farmall Hs were sold on rubber, this 1940 example, owned by John and Mary Lou Poch of New Holstein, Wisconsin, has the optional steel.

Turbulent Times in the Tractor Business

"What? What's that? How much? Two-hundred-and-thirty dollars? Well, I'll be . . . What'll we do about it? Do? Why damn it all, meet him, of course! We're going to stay in the tractor business. Yes, cut two-hundred-and-thirty dollars. Both models. Yes, both. And, say, listen, make it good! We'll throw in a plow as well."

That is half of a 1922 telephone conversation between International Harvester's Chicago and Springfield, Ohio, offices. The words are those of Alexander Legge, the company's gritty general manager, as recorded by Cyrus McCormick III in his book *The Century of the Reaper*. The occasion was a salvo fired by Henry Ford in the great tractor war of the twenties. He had just announced a price cut to $395 for the Fordson tractor.

McCormick's grandfather had countered the loss of his reaper patent protection by branching out into other implement areas. His heirs likewise recovered their loss of supremacy in the binder and harvester arenas at the time of consolidation into International Harvester by branching out into tractors. Wrote McCormick, "The harvester war of the Eighteen-Nineties was cruel, disastrous to the weaker

Introduced in 1939, the Farmall H was originally sold with steel wheels for about $750. Some opted for rubber front tires and steel rears, for a price of about $775. Full rubber raised the price to about $950.

combatants, and yet it was inspiring in the way its testing brought out the finer qualities of men. But in the first twenty International years, competition had perhaps become routine. Henry Ford's presence in the implement province and the new type of competition he soon introduced returned the industry for a time to the atmosphere of battle."

Since its formation in 1902 until after World War I, International Harvester Company had been under constant legal attack. This was an era when trust busting was a fashionable thing for politicians and lawyers to be engaged in, and some considered the merging of several companies to form International Harvester to be a patent attempt to eliminate competition. Several states, at least for a short time, forbade International Harvester to do business within their borders. All this culminated in about 1918 with the sale of three of the companies comprising International Harvester and the elimination of dual (McCormick and Deering) dealerships. Having survived all that, McCormick's heirs now found themselves under a strong, competitive attack.

By the end of World War I, International Harvester's "full-line" competitors were proving increasingly able, especially in the tractor market. Chief competitors included Massey-Harris, Case, and Deere, just entering the tractor fray in 1919 with the purchase of the Waterloo Boy outfit. There were also many short-line, or tractor-only,

competitors, including in 1917 one Henry Ford of automobile fame.

Ford was raised on a farm and empathized with the hard-working, under-paid, and mostly unappreciated farmer. He was concerned especially for the eastern and midwestern small farmer trying to wrest a living often from fewer than 80 acres. Ford, who never cared much for horses stated, "The burden of farming must be lifted from flesh and blood and placed on steel and motors."

Ford intended his tractor to do for the farmer what his Model T car had done—that is, free him from bondage to the horse. The tractor was to be made by a separate company from the car company (which was then stockholder-owned) called Henry Ford and Son. The "Son" part was to signify the inclusion of his young son, Edsel. The tractor, therefore, was to be named the "Fordson."

Thanks to the postwar economic depression, Ford soon found himself with more tractors than he could sell, and so he started cutting prices to move inventory. The early twenties market continued to shrink, further exacerbating the then-industry-wide overproduction problem. Other producers, eager to maintain market share, also cut prices, and soon found themselves em-

A slightly scaled-down version of the mighty Farmall M was the Farmall H. The H used a 152ci engine, rather than the 248ci engine of the M. Wheelbases and frame mountings were the same, however, allowing the use of the same mounted implements. Standard rear tires were 10x36; fronts were 5.50x16. The H could comfortably handle a 22in threshing machine.

broiled in a good old-fashioned price war.

The tractor price war had three prominent effects. First, many farmers took advantage of the below-cost prices to get into power farming. Second, substantial companies were eliminated from the tractor market when they could not get their prices down sufficiently to compete—mainly the short-line companies specializing in larger,

heavier tractors. Finally, the survivors were forced to copy Ford's production-line methods and to redesign their products to be more appealing to the myriad of smaller farmers.

In 1920, *Farm Machinery and Equipment* magazine listed 166 tractor companies, which produced slightly more than 200,000 tractors. That year, Ford produced 54,000 Fordsons in Dearborn and 43,000 in Cork, Ireland. Obviously, Ford was the competition, and only International Harvester had the strength to take him on.

The Fordson had been launched in late 1917. At first, the industry didn't take it seriously. One Philip C. Rose, writer of the *Black Book*, dismissed the Fordson as inconsequential, saying that the other tractor manufacturers need not worry about Ford. "His machine," Rose said of Ford's Fordson, "will not stand up; that he will find in short order."

The tractor "gurus" of the time disdained the Fordson for several reasons. First, Ford's claim to fame was the Model T car. While the Model T did put America on wheels, it also spawned a whole new lingo of expletives. About the kindest thing to be said about the "Tin Lizzie" was that it was cheap. One thing the tractor gurus missed, however, was that the Model T really did quite well on the semi-improved rural roads, and it soon was a favorite of the beleaguered small farmer. In addition, because of Ford's apparent concern for the "little guy" (as demonstrated by his five-dollar-a-day pay for assembly-line work), many people lauded Henry Ford as a kind of saint.

Second, the Fordson was ridiculously small and light. At 2700lb, it was dwarfed by other new tractors of the times, such as the 6000lb Waterloo Boy or the 8700lb IHC Titan.

Finally, Ford was not in the farm implement business. The most prosperous tractor suppliers also made such equipment as threshers, spreaders, mowers, and the like.

What the tractor gurus failed to anticipate was that Ford would distribute the tractors through his extensive automobile dealer network. He issued quotas for each; even big city dealers had to take their share, doing anything to get rid of them.

Furthermore, World War I had just begun, and even though Ford was a pacifist, he generously made a gift of the patent rights to the Fordson to the British Board of Agriculture. He also agreed to set up a factory to produce them in Cork, Ireland, and, in 1918, shipped 6,000 Fordsons to Great Britain to help alleviate the wartime food shortage.

It was these, 6,000 exported Fordsons that brought the tractor its credibility. In these days before Nebraska Tractor Tests, there was not much a farmer could do to assure himself of a tractor's viability. In Great Britain, in addition to the Fordson, several other makes of tractors were pressed into service. Objective comparisons could be made. The British County War Agricultural Committees hired drivers and paid for repairs and fuel, and kept records of acres plowed per hour and of associated costs. According to Michael Williams, in his book *Ford and Fordson Tractors*, the Fordson could plow more acres per hour than either the Titan or the Waterloo Boy, and do it at less cost for fuel and repairs.

Now Fordson production took off. Production numbers for the two plants

in Dearborn and Cork topped 90,000 in 1920, more than most tractor models saw as a lifetime run. By 1921, however, the postwar depression caused sales to drop to fewer than 37,000. Henry Ford's tractor "engine" was running, though, and a way had to be found to move more tractors. Thus, the prices were cut throughout the year from $700 to $625, and finally down to $395: Ford was testing the elasticity of demand. In any case, Fordsons sold. The year 1922 saw production back to around the 70,000-unit level, and in 1923, to more than 100,000.

International Harvester first countered with the 10-20 McCormick-Deering in 1922, a smaller version of the 15-30 introduced in 1921. Others, such as Case and John Deere, brought out new, smaller, lighter, less-expensive models as well. Nevertheless, Ford carried more than 60 percent of the market. Competition from the Fordson eliminated many companies from the field over the next several years, including the mighty General Motors' entry, the Samson.

By 1929, the great tractor war was over. Of the 166 listed for 1920, there were only forty-seven tractor manufacturers left, and they were still producing just slightly more than 200,000 units. By then, both the Fordson and the Model T were also gone from the scene. Henry Ford said he stopped production of the Fordson because he needed the space to begin construction of the new Model A car, brought out in 1928 to replace the Model T. But the facts are that the Fordson, as well as the Model T, had been overtaken by determined competition: In the case of the Model T, it was the Chevrolet automobile, and in the case of the Fordson, it was the Farmall tractor, introduced by International Harvester in 1924.

Chapter 1

In the Beginning

During the early part of the nineteenth century, transportation, communication, power for manufacturing, and financial facilities were nothing at all like we enjoy today. It was a time of dramatic change, a time now known as the Industrial Revolution, fueled by the appearance of several interrelated inventions. George Stephenson in Great Britain and Robert Fulton in America showed the world how to use the power of steam for transportation. Samuel Morse invented the telegraph; Eli Whitney, the cotton gin; Elias Howe, the sewing machine; Henry Bessemer, the steel-making process; Cyrus McCormick, the reaper; and John Pope, the threshing machine. None of these inventions by themselves would have amounted to much. But together, they synergistically facilitated each other's development—and

The Farmall M, introduced in August of 1939, was without a doubt International Harvester's most famous tractor. More than 288,000 were sold before production ended in 1952. Configurations included various high-crop and wide-front versions; shown here is a 1940 vintage M on full steel. The most powerful member of the Farmall clan, the mighty M was a three- or four-bottom plow tractor. In most cases, the smooth four-cylinder power of the M could handle a 30in thresher. Although most Farmall Ms were delivered with rubber tires, this 1940 example is on full steel, a popular option in those days.

ultimately led to the birth of machinery factories.

Work became less labor-intensive as industry was taken out of the home workshop and transferred to these factories. Automation replaced handwork in every area of life. Skilled specialists managed the great new enterprises, and marketing became national, rather than local and regional.

Especially in agriculture, invention sparked further invention, as farmers modified existing or developed new machines to make their lives easier. In this way, International Harvester was formed mainly out of Cyrus McCormick's and William Deering's implement companies, companies that resulted from efforts to invent and perfect new grain-harvesting machinery.

It is mind-boggling to consider the physical labor needed to produce a loaf of bread at any time before the turn of the nineteenth century. First, the soil was tilled with a primitive plow or spade, and then, the seed was sown by hand. Next, the grain was cut by sickle or scythe. Finally, the grain was threshed from the stalk with a flail, and the chaff and straw were winnowed from the grain—a laborious process indeed. All this had to be done before the grain could be milled into flour for baking. There had to be an easier way.

As early as the first century A.D., attempts were made to mechanize the task of collecting, or reaping, grain. These early efforts took the form of

The Farmall M used a large 248ci four-cylinder overhead-valve engine, operating at 1450rpm. Bore and stroke were 3.88x 5.25in. The standard rear tires were 11.25x36; the fronts were 6.50x16. Weights of up to 7000lb with ballast were common.

head-strippers: usually a box on wheels or runners and pushed by oxen into the standing grain. The leading upper edge

of the box was a metal bar with sharp, tapered slots. As the contraption advanced, the stalks entered the slots and the "ears" were stripped and fell into the box behind. At least that is what happened in theory. The fact that these stripping harvesters did little to replace the scythe, or even the reaping hook, is testimony to their inefficiency.

An Englishman by the name of Salmon did, however, invent a mowing

machine consisting of two serrated cutter bars, one on top of the other and oscillating in opposite directions. Projecting fingers in front of the cutter bars were used to hold the stalks against the cutters. Salmon's machine also used a "divider" bar, which separated the stand to be cut from that to be left for the next pass.

The Pioneers

Cyrus Hall McCormick was born to Robert and Mary Ann McCormick on February 15, 1809. Robert was by then a fairly wealthy Virginia farmer, with more than 500 acres of land. His estate had its own grist mill, sawmill, smelter, distillery, and blacksmith shop. An imaginative man with mechanical ingenuity, Robert tinkered with the invention of a mechanical reaper as early as 1809, but success was to wait for his son. Robert did succeed, as did his British counterparts, in making a workable grain cutter, but, as with the British machines, it left the grain stalks too tangled for binding. Son Cyrus was no doubt party to these endeavors as he was growing up and, in July 1831, demonstrated the first truly successful reaping machine.

The McCormick reaper used a sickle bar after the fashion of the Salmon cutter, with the fingers projecting out front to hold the stalks at the moment of cutting. It had the sweep reel of the British Ogle and Bell machines and it used the divider of the Salmon machine. McCormick's device had three unique features: a platform onto which the grain fell, to then be raked off onto the ground in bunches suitable for bundling; the horse, and hence the line of draft, placed off to one side, thereby allowing the horse to walk in the stubble of the swath already cut, rather than trample the standing grain; and one main wheel, which operated the cutter and carried the machine, mounted directly behind the horse in the line of draft. Two men and a horse with a McCormick reaper could harvest about an acre per hour.

McCormick sold a few reapers along the lines of his first model, but

farmers were not clamoring for them. Most considered them to be curiosities. American farms of the 1830s were not sufficiently developed to be free of stumps, humps, and rocks, and farmers were skeptical of the machine's ability to work under these conditions. McCormick also found some of the reticence encountered by his British counterparts—that is, a resentment by farm laborers who thought that these machines would throw them out of work.

Besides the lack of a market for reapers, Cyrus McCormick and his father found their interests diverted to other pursuits at this time. They were involved in other farm inventions and manufacturing activities—one of which was the McCormick cast-iron plow, which sold well before the steel plow was invented. And while their interests were elsewhere, a Mr. Obed Hussey secured, in 1833, the first US patent for a reaping machine.

The Hussey patent jolted Cyrus's attention back to reapers. He immediately filed for his own patent, which was granted in 1834. Thus began a bitter conflict that lasted for years.

A McCormick BWD6 with owner Churchill and his dog Flick at the great Dorset Steam Fair near Blandford, England. In 1954, the BMD was replaced by the BWD6. Possibly for marketing reasons, they were not described as "Standards." The International Harvester Company in Great Britain expanded its production facilities into the old Jowett car and van works at Idle, Bradford.

Hussey's reaper was somewhat different from McCormick's in that it had two drive wheels, plus smaller wheels to carry the cutter; it used no reel, and side delivery was not provided. The

17

binder had to keep up with the machine so that the sheaves would be out of the way before it came around again. The main advantage of the Hussey reaper was the open-top guard finger

bar that allowed chaff and other debris to exit, instead of plugging up and jamming the cutter.

The War of the Reapers

By 1840, McCormick was beginning to enter the market in earnest. Due to some unfortunate changes, the popularity of the Hussey reaper was beginning to wane. Feeling the pressure of competition, Hussey challenged McCormick to a field trial, and by 1843, Hussey and McCormick agreed to a public contest, to be held in the James River area of Virginia. Each machine was to harvest similar plots of the same field; the first one done was the winner. In two events, McCormick's reaper finished first, partly because of mechanical problems with the Hussey machine and partly due to the more difficult binding configuration wherein the binders had to keep up with the machine.

Hussey continued to challenge McCormick in the field and in the courtroom until his death in 1860 in a railroad accident. Unfortunately for both men, their patents expired at just about the same time that mechanical reaping was gaining wide acceptance with farmers. Mechanical reaping really caught on when the self-raker came on the market. Later, came the self-tying binders that made all the old reapers obsolete.

Severe competition continued throughout the rest of the nineteenth century as each of the major concerns tried to be the first to acquire the manufacturing rights to promising new inventions. Armies of machinery agents tromped across rural America searching for customers to fight over—with the salesmen sometimes coming to blows. Advertising and promotional budgets soared. And when a sale was made, the salesman feted the customer lavishly. Often, the farmer's entire family would be invited to town to take delivery of the machine, and then honored with a grand restaurant meal. On one occasion, a McCormick agent had several machines to deliver on a certain day. He hired three bands, had floats made, and had a parade, with the customers riding in fancy carriages.

The McCormick Harvesting Machine Company

By 1847, the McCormick Harvesting Machine Company of Walnut Grove Farm, Virginia, had already been in business for more than seven years. Like both John Deere and J. I. Case, Cyrus McCormick recognized that the market for grain harvesting equipment was farther west and decided to move his operations to the frontier town of Chicago. On August 30, 1847, McCormick entered into a partnership with C. M. Gray of Chicago. While McCormick was away from Chicago, Gray sold half of his half-interest in the new company to Messrs. Ogden and Jones. Needless to say, McCormick was upset over the arrangement and took Gray to court. While the matter was awaiting decision, Gray sold the remaining portion of his interest to Ogden. Thus, in 1848, the business was renamed McCormick, Ogden and Company, with Jones still a junior partner. By September of the next year, Ogden and Jones sold their interests to McCormick for $65,000.

To help him run his burgeoning business, Cyrus invited his brothers, Leander and William, to come to Chicago. Things went well until William died in 1865, and acrimony arose over the distribution of his estate. Cyrus and Leander did not get along well from then on. In 1879, the partnership was converted into a corporation, with Cyrus holding three-fourths of the stock and Leander, the balance.

Next page
John Poch's Farmall 450 has the optional torque amplifier, which has ten forward speeds and two reverse, rather than the standard five and one. This tractor also has the optional adjustable wide front. John has fabricated a three-point hitch for it. It has no muffler so John can fit it into his garage. The Farmall 450 diesel is essentially the same as the 400, except for a 281ci four-cylinder engine instead of the 264ci.

Farmall Super M production ran from 1952 to 1954, replacing the M, which itself replaced the F-30 in 1939. The engine of the Super M displaced 264ci, up from 248ci for the M and down from 284ci for the F-30.

Cyrus H. McCormick died in 1884, after witnessing the great revolution in mechanized agriculture, after acquiring great wealth, and after seeing his reaper company grow to become the largest of its kind. His widow and his son, Cyrus Jr., bought out Leander's interest in 1890. By this time, however, the company's preeminence in the field was being seriously challenged, because McCormick had been too slow in picking up promising new invention rights—the slowness due in the most part to the bickering between the brothers.

Deering Company

William Deering was one of those to capitalize on McCormick's slowness. McCormick had been in the reaper business for about forty years when Deering, then forty-four years old, bought into the rights to the Marsh harvester.

Before entering the implement business, Deering had made a substantial fortune in the wholesale dry goods business in Maine. In 1870, he made his way to Chicago to invest in some land, but happened to call on an acquaintance named Elijah Gammon, a retired Methodist preacher, who had become a partner in the firm that was attempting to manufacture the Marsh harvester. Gammon persuaded Deering to look no further for investments, but to put his money into the harvester company. When, two years later, the books showed that Deering had doubled his money, he asked to be taken into the business as a partner. By the next year, poor health caused Gammon to call for Deering to move to Chicago and take over management of the business. In 1880, Gammon sold out to Deering.

The idea of amalgamation, wrote Cyrus Hall McCormick III, was first broached between McCormick, Sr., and Deering before the former's death in 1884. Nothing came of it, however, because the temperaments of those first-generation harvester men were too individualistic. After the death of C. H. McCormick, Sr., the records are full of accounts of meetings called to consider merger, meetings that included other smaller implement companies. The smaller companies recognized that the kind of competition that had flourished would be ruinous for all concerned, and so wanted, at least, an understanding on pricing.

The American Harvester Company

By 1890, McCormick and Deering were the commanding leaders in the harvesting industry. Deering, by now getting on in years, encouraged consolidation. In the fall of 1890, the McCormicks, the Deerings, and eighteen other competitors met in Chicago to attempt the industry's first amalgamation. What emerged was an industrial giant, the American Harvester Company. The six chief shareholders elected themselves directors, with Cyrus McCormick, Jr., as president and the aging Deering as chairman.

The American Harvester Company was doomed from the start. At that time, all the harvesting companies bought their knives and cutters from the Akron, Ohio, firm Whitman, Barnes Company. Its president, Colonel A. L. Conger, conceived the idea for the American Harvester Company in such a way that guaranteed the preservation of his own little concern. For several years before the grand Chicago merger meeting, on sales trips, Colonel Conger enthusiastically discussed the idea with all his customers. His mistake was in encouraging the smaller entrepreneurs to establish the economic valuation of their own companies, without benefit of formal appraisal, and these were the values attributed when the consolidation occurred.

While the valuation of the new company was high, banks saw through the scheme and refused to lend working capital. McCormick and Deering also balked at supplying the funding for what they saw as weaker competitors—and the short-lived American Harvester Company foundered. The government was also threatening involvement under the newly passed Sherman Antitrust Act, as it clearly saw the consolidation as restraint of trade.

For the next decade, the industry vacillated between merger and ruinous competition. Deering proposed, in 1897, to sell out to Cyrus McCormick, Jr., but McCormick was unable to raise the cash. Vigorous competition resumed, with Deering continuing to gain on McCormick's leadership.

The International Harvester Company

The years 1896 and 1897 saw a severe recession in American business, due in large extent to over-saturation of

markets through devastating price wars. Companies reacted by merging to eliminate competition as the economy recovered. Between 1898 and 1902, 212 consolidations occurred, almost twice the number from the preceding nine years.

The two harvesting dynasties now became serious about getting together. Deering proposed a two-step merger: Each family should buy minority interest in the other firm, and then, together, they would acquire three other competitors, Plano Manufacturing of Chicago; Warder, Bushnell & Glessner of Springfield, Ohio; and Milwaukee Harvester Company of Milwaukee, Wisconsin.

The McCormicks, still the strongest, balked at any suggestion of loss of control. The merger efforts almost stalled until George W. Perkins, a J. P. Morgan partner and adviser to the McCormicks, proposed a ten-year stock trust. The trust would hold all of the stock of the new International Harvester Company, with Perkins, McCormick, and Charles Deering (William's son) serving as trustees.

Thus, after more than ten years of cat-and-mouse play, on July 28, 1902, International Harvester Company was born. The name, picked by George Perkins, was selected to reflect its global scope. Harvester, as it came to be called, controlled 85 percent of US harvester production and boasted assets of $110 million (a staggering amount in 1902). Included were malleable iron works, twine factories, timberland and sawmills, hemp properties, coal and iron mines, and the Illinois Northern Railway—plus the plants in Chicago, Milwaukee, and Springfield.

The stockholders of the new concern had every reason to be confident, and they were not disappointed. Although profit margins were small at first, the company's monopolistic position, its reputation for producing good equipment, and its strong dealer network assured success. There were still many serious internal struggles, however. It was fortunate that Perkins was

able to override the petty squabbles between the McCormick and the Deering factions. He became disgusted with Harvester's "millionaire officers" who refused to work or follow orders, and was finally able to promote from within Clarence Funk to general manager, a capable professional executive with ties to neither family.

After the voting trust set up by Perkins expired, the McCormicks borrowed $5 million from John D. Rockefeller to regain control. Rather than reinstate their rather inept management, however, the McCormick family kept Perkins's idea of professional management. Their first move after regaining control was to fire Funk and replace him with a McCormick loyalist, Alexander Legge.

The talented Legge, who had worked himself up from a position in a field office collecting bad debts from farmers, was one of the key players in the events that followed. It was his vision that resulted in the Farmall tractor—the tractor that saved the company during the great tractor war of the twenties.

Chapter 2

Birth of the Farmall

In 1769, James Watt of Great Britain obtained a patent on a steam engine that used a separate condenser, thus recovering much of the water. This device made the steam engine practical for propelling ships and trains. Watt, therefore, is generally credited with inventing the steam engine, although expansion engines date back to more than 100 years before the birth of Christ.

The steam traction engine was the first step in power farming. One of the first more-or-less successful of these was the Fawkes Steam Plow, made in 1858. Others followed in short order, but all were big, heavy, and expensive, suitable for only the largest farms.

Then in 1876, Nikolaus August Otto invented the four-stroke-cycle internal-combustion engine—no small task, considering that spark plugs, carburetors, and ignition systems had not yet been created. Such pioneers as Daimler, Benz, Duryea, Olds, and Ford soon took the "Otto Cycle" engine out of the novelty realm. Powered buggies of all sorts began to appear.

The first successful Otto Cycle-powered traction engine was built by John Froelich of Froelich, Iowa, in 1892. It could be considered a hybrid because Froelich used a Robinson steam engine frame and running gear upon which he mounted a Van Duzen one-cylinder engine. The machine had an operator's platform in front and a steering wheel, and could propel itself backward and forward. The 20hp engine was operated on gasoline, a fuel that a short time before had been considered a hazardous by-product of the lubricating oil business.

During the 1892 harvest season, Froelich used the machine in a fifty-day custom threshing operation. He both pulled and powered a Case 40x58 thresher, harvesting approximately 72,000 bushels of small grain. A year later, Froelich was instrumental in forming the Waterloo Gasoline Traction Engine Company of Waterloo, Iowa. This company went on to produce the Waterloo Boy tractor, the forerunner of the John Deere line.

Early efforts of the Waterloo Gasoline Traction Engine Company did not, however, produce a commercially viable tractor. That honor goes to two men of Charles City, Iowa: Charles Hart and Charles Parr. As a youth, Hart, who grew up near Charles City, dreamed of motorized farming, and methodically began achieving his goal. As a young man, he enrolled in Iowa

For its production timeframe (1952–1954), the Super M was in the "big league" as far as power was concerned. The big league for row-crop tractors in those days was the more than 40hp class. In its Nebraska tests, the various M versions averaged 45 maximum belt horsepower. In its class were the Allis Chalmers WD-45 (45hp), the Cockshutt 50 (50hp), the John Deere 70 (46hp), the Massey-Harris 44 (45hp), and the Oliver Super 88 (54hp). Dan Langy of Lena, Illinois, operates this 1952 example.

This early, 1927 Farmall advertisement stressed that the Farmall was an all-purpose tractor.

State College of Agriculture and Mechanical Arts. He soon discovered that the professors did not share his enthusiasm for power farming, and transferred to the University of Wisconsin, where he not only found a more congenial faculty, but also met another talented engineering student, Charles Parr, who soon joined him in his mechanized farming dream.

While still students, they formed the Hart-Parr Gasoline Engine Company, and began manufacturing engines for sale. Upon graduation, they moved their operations to Charles City and began work on the traction engine. In 1902, they completed their first unit, one that from the outset was designed for drawbar work. Consequently, the transmission and drivetrain were extremely rugged.

By 1907, one-third of all tractors (about 600) at work in the United States were Hart-Parrs. In fact, a Hart-Parr employee is credited with coining the word "tractor," saying that "traction engine" seemed too cumbersome for use in advertising.

International Harvester Tractors

The William Deering Company made its first gasoline engine in 1891, a 6hp two-cylinder device. Also available were 12hp and 16hp versions, which were used on self-propelled corn pickers and mowers.

McCormick's first venture into the engine business was in 1897 with a two-cylinder engine installed on a running gear. It used a two-speed transmission, with reverse.

After International Harvester was formed in 1902, interest in and work on tractors accelerated. Harvester was among the first of the long-line implement companies to offer a tractor, the first of which was introduced in 1906.

Early design was faulty. A single-cylinder engine was mounted on rollers so that it could be moved back and forth to engage a friction drive. The engine had an open crankcase and used spray-tank cooling. This tractor was initially built in Upper Sandusky, Ohio, but the plant soon moved, first to Akron and then to Milwaukee.

With the second move, the friction drive was replaced by a clutch and gearbox. By 1910, International Harvester overtook Hart-Parr and became the nation's leading tractor producer. Only a few thousand tractors were produced each year in the whole country: they were expensive, being essentially shop-built, and were extremely large. Also, only a small market existed at the time, as most farmers could neither use nor afford such monstrosities.

Nevertheless, other farm equipment suppliers jumped on the slow-moving tractor bandwagon, and soon overproduction swamped the market.

The office of the 1913 45hp Titan.

Other names—Rumely, Avery, J. I. Case, Aultman-Taylor, and Minneapolis—soon graced internal-combustion tractors. Smaller companies with good ideas also entered the fray. In 1910, Harvester added its Mogul to the lineup. Most of these tractors reflected the heritage of the steam engine; some even looked like steamers. Their average weight was more than 500lb per engine horsepower.

The Tractor Takes On the Horse

The giant tractors built before 1915, both steam- and gasoline-powered, were built for two purposes: driving the ever-larger threshing machines and busting the virgin prairie sod in the Canadian and US Great Plains. Farm publications and Department of Agriculture studies touted the advantages of power farming. All recognized the problem: the tractor would only be viable for the average farmer when it could replace horses.

Records indicate that some families in those days actually subsisted on farms of fewer than forty acres. The farther west one went, the larger the farms were, on average. Even in the 1940s, most farms east of the Mississippi River were fewer than 100 acres. Required horsepower averaged about one horse, ox, or mule for every fifteen acres under cultivation. And the animal ate the produce of at least three acres.

There were at least perceived advantages to animal power over the tractor. Animals provided fertilizer and hides for leather; bones and hoofs were also used. And there was an affectionate bond between it and the farmer; the hours of toiling together and in sharing in the harvest resulted in a bonding between human and animal that tran-

Power farming was not for the faint of heart—or those with a small wallet. This mammoth J. I. Case steam engine plowing a demonstration plot pulling a twelve-bottom plow was typical of power farming at the turn of the century.

An International Harvester Mogul 10-20 tractor on display at the Living History Antique Equipment Show in Franklin Grove, Illinois. The Mogul 10-20 was manufactured between 1916 and 1919. Mogul tractors were sold by McCormick dealers; more than 8,900 were built. It had a single-cylinder engine with a bore and stroke of 8.50x12.00in. A two-speed transmission was featured, along with a roller-chain final drive. The engine operated on kerosene, with water injection available for hard pulls and hot days. The engine was started on gasoline. Three needle valves, convenient to the driver, controlled the flow of gasoline, kerosene, and water.

A McCormick-Deering 15-30 Gear Drive Tractor pulls a self-powered McCormick-Deering combine through a Kansas wheatfield in the 1920s. The 15-30 was the first International tractor with a one-piece cast-iron frame, introduced in 1921. Smithsonian Institution

scended that which a person might have for a pet. Following World War I, animal advocates derided and denounced the concept of the horseless farm, solemnly predicting various evils that would befall the nation.

There was one big advantage to horse power over horsepower: with the horse, there were no new models and no new ways to learn. As a person grew up on a farm, they learned without any special training how to handle the draft animals. With the tractor, he or she had to "learn to drive." A whole new technology had to be learned, and with the rapid pace of progress, the goal of mastering it kept moving out ahead. The farmer before the 1930s saw the time it would take to learn to use this laborsaving device and scoffed at it as, rather, a labor-causing device.

Smaller and Lighter Tractors

After 1912, to appeal to the smaller farmer, tractor designers sought to make smaller, lighter, and cheaper tractors—machinery versatile enough to replace the horse in at least some farm tasks, reducing the total number required on the farm.

The next year, the Bull Tractor Company introduced a 12hp single-wheel-drive tractor, selling for around $400. This trim, agile little device rattled the industry as it out-maneuvered the doddering behemoths it competed against. While it was never mechanically sound, it did sweep the

A 1913 45hp Titan by International Harvester. The Titan brand tractors were made for sale by Deering dealers. Titan was an appropriate name for this 21,000lb monster. It readily handled a 14in ten-bottom plow. At the Winnipeg Competition, it demonstrated a 2.54 acres-per-hour plowing rate. The unusual two-cylinder engine was started by compressed air and drove its own compressor. The engine was unusual in that the side-by-side pistons operated together on the same crank throw, rather than opposite, as do most other two-cylinder engines. Being a four-stroke engine, this gave even firing, once per revolution. This Titan is owned by the American Thresherman's Association and was displayed at the Central States Thresherman's Reunion near Pontiac, Illinois.

This prewar Farmall ad uses the cartoon approach. Note in the third box the reference to the fact that the "team is getting old. . . ." The horse was a major competitor to the Farmall in 1941.

field of customers, being first in sales (displacing International Harvester) by 1914. Its popularity did not last long, but it did spawn a subsidiary much in evidence today: Toro, the lawn, garden, and golf course equipment maker.

With the advent of smaller, lighter tractors, the farmer received an additional benefit: the farmer could convert horse-drawn implements to tractor use, thereby saving considerably on cost. Many of these implements did not fully use the tractor's capability, and others were simply not strong enough to stand up, but the transition to power farming was being made.

The rapid rise of the automobile also affected the tractor industry as advances brought by large production

trickled down. Automobile use proliferated tenfold between 1910 and 1925. As farmers availed themselves of the benefits of the automobile, they also became more comfortable with the tractor—especially a smaller tractor that had features and controls similar to those of the car.

Persistent borrowing of automobile technology indicated to many that the tractor had more in common with the automobile than with other implements such as plows and threshers. Therefore, it did not take a great leap of faith to believe rumors as early as 1914 that Henry Ford was about to get into the tractor business.

Ford had been experimenting with "automobile plows" as early as 1906. One effect of the Ford rumors was that a group of Minneapolis entrepreneurs, which included a man by the name of Ford, organized the Ford Tractor Company, attempting to capitalize on the magic name. Although this outfit did actually make and sell a few tractors, their efforts, like their tractors, were short-lived.

The Minneapolis Ford tractor had less of an impact on power farming than did a spate of Model T Ford car-to-tractor conversion kits available at the time. C. H. Wendel lists forty-five such kit manufacturers, as of 1919, in his book *Encyclopedia of American Farm Tractors*.

These kits, which were advertised as being easy to install and remove, usually included large lugged wheels to be mounted on a frame extension with chain reduction drives from the regular axles. Costing around $200, these kits did fill the bill for many a two- to three-horse farmer, but their usefulness was definitely limited. The Model T itself, however, did quite well under these trying circumstances, further endearing it to the hapless small farmer. Henry Ford must have relished the publicity garnered for his Model T, and in no way discouraged the kit-makers.

The Advent of the Fordson

With the impeccable timing, the Fordson burst on the scene on October

8, 1917. Although fewer than 300 were made that year, the concept of the light, small, mass-produced, and inexpensive tractor was realized.

The timing was right because of the civil and social turmoil then boiling up in Europe and soon to involve America. American farmers saw an increase in produce prices as much of Europe was taken out of production because of the war. The war also required the services of farmhands and horses. Both draftees and draft animals went off to war in record numbers, leaving the farmers with little choice but to use the laborsaving tractor.

European governments sought large-scale shipments of American tractors to stave off food shortages; this is when Henry Ford committed much of the 1918 Fordson production to Great Britain. There is no question that the Fordson had Harvester on the ropes in 1922, but when the going got tough, Harvester's management brought in a tough engineer.

Enter Edward A. Johnston

The competition the Fordson stirred up provided the incentive to develop a machine that could do what the Fordson could not. The Fordson was not useful for cultivating such crops as corn and cotton; it did not have a driveshaft power takeoff and, therefore was not suitable for the new harvesting implements; and, most of all, it could replace some horses on a farm, but not all of them.

As early as 1910, Harvester engineers had talked to General Manager Alexander Legge about a more ver-

A 1929 Farmall Regular, Serial Number T70344, owned by John and Mary Lou Poch, of New Holstein, Wisconsin. The Farmall pioneered the configuration of the dual-narrow-front, row-crop tractor, with the steering rod over the top of the engine. The steering rod engages the vertical steering post through a gear mesh. The Farmall also pioneered frame mounting points for mounted implements.

satile tractor. The head of the Experimental Department at the time was a young engineer with an irrepressible spirit named Edward A. Johnston.

Johnston had started with the McCormick outfit during the harvester war of the 1890s. He had been instrumental in keeping McCormick's products competitive with patents covering mowers, knotters, binders, headers,

The classic Farmall styling, by famous industrial designer Raymond Loewy, remained in production between 1939 and 1957. This example, a 1952 Super M, shows the timeless beauty of form and function.

and the like. Johnston's activities with motor vehicles began with a machine he made for himself before the turn of the century, which he dubbed the "Auto Buggy." For many years, he used it to commute between his home and the plant. In the early 1900s, Cyrus McCormick became interested in the Auto Buggy and commissioned Johnston to make one after the fashion of a farm wagon, capable of hauling a ton of cargo. This machine appeared on the market in 1906 and was the forerunner of the International truck.

Farmall F-12 production began in 1932, but only twenty-five were built that year. More than 123,000 were built before production ended in 1937.

Johnston and his team, which included such geniuses as Bert R. Benjamin and C. W. Mott, had some ideas for improving the tractor's utility—including the development of an all-purpose tractor. As development progressed, they kept General Manager Legge and Chairman McCormick informed, but the company expressed no official interest.

That changed in July 1921, when the Fordson threatened the whole International Harvester empire. Legge called in Johnston and asked him what had happened to the ten, or so, all-purpose tractor designs. By then, John-

ston and his team had focused on one type, of which several prototypes existed. Johnston insisted that this all-purpose "Farmall" could beat the Fordson in every way. When told this, Legge immediately ordered the construction of twenty more hand-built examples. He also ordered a full complement of implements to be customized for the Farmall. Both were to be ready for thorough testing in 1922.

Legge and Johnston resisted the temptation to rush the Farmall into production despite the rising menace of the Fordson. The engineers worked out design problems for both performance and mass production. Numerous patents were obtained. A third generation of test prototypes was built and tested. In 1924, 200 preproduction models were sold. Harvester field representatives watched closely as farmers put the new Farmall through its paces under actual conditions. Feedback to the design team resulted in a few more changes to the tractor and implements and in many new implements. Estimates acquired by the field representatives indicated a sixfold reduction in planting, tilling, and harvesting costs versus horse farming.

Farmall sales exceeded expectations in 1925. By 1926, the new Rock Island, Illinois, plant was in operation and Farmalls were rolling out the door. The Farmall then drove the lowly Fordson from the field.

Even at its peak production, before the crash of 1929, only about 24,000 Farmalls were built each year, a far cry from the 100,000 Fordsons built during Ford's peak years. By the end of the 1920s, International Harvester Company was clearly again at the top of the long-line farm implement industry. It enjoyed sales three times that of its nearest competitor, Deere & Company of Moline, Illinois.

The introduction of the Farmall was an enormous triumph for Harvester not only because of its victory over the Fordson. It also overcame sticky resistance to the concept of the all-purpose tractor both within the company and in the industry at large. When the first Farmall rolled out, there was no advertising blitz, no ceremony, not even a press conference. Harvester management was so cautious that initially sales were to be made only in Texas to prevent corporate embarrassment if they were not successful. An article in the March 1931 issue of *Agricultural Engineering* recounts the situation: "No development in the industry was regarded with more distrust and wholesale opposition than the suggested general-purpose tractor. . . . The opposition came more from farm implement manufacturers' home organizations than from the field, and those organizations certainly deserve credit for their relentless efforts to have this type of tractor released for experimental development. . . ."

When the Farmall appeared, it seemed top-heavy and fragile-looking compared to standard-tread tractors of its day. The Farmall and its imitators sold so well that they changed the concept of the conventional tractor to that of the row-crop configuration. This remained so into the 1960s when chemical herbicides replaced the need for crop cultivators and wide-fronts again became popular. With the current interest in ecological safeguards, the tractor cultivator may again be used to fight weeds.

To say that the Farmall was a success would be an understatement. The farmers loved this tractor. Most, however, hedged their bets and kept their horses for another season. Few did after the first year. Sales of the new tractor, while not disappointing, were low because farmers did not have the necessary cash. Lack of real faith in the Farmall by company management also left the production facilities somewhat strained and prevented lowering of the price through the full impact of true mass production. Nevertheless, the Farmall assembled well, worked well on the farm, sold well, and made a profit for the stockholders.

The surviving competitors quickly joined the all-purpose tractor field, but International Harvester enjoyed unchallenged tractor leadership until, in 1939, Henry Ford again redefined the word "tractor" with the introduction of the Ford-Ferguson 9N.

Chapter 3

Development of the Farmall Tractor

The configuration of the new Farmall tractor is generally credited to Bert R. Benjamin. In 1921, when International Harvester General Manager Alexander Legge commissioned the all-purpose tractor, Benjamin was superintendent of the McCormick Works' Experimental Division.

Harvester engineers had been experimenting with various tractor and motor cultivator configurations since 1910. Other tractor makers were struggling with unconventional approaches to the problem of replacing the horse. Many unusual configurations (which now seem ridiculous) were built, tested, and even sold.

After the appearance of the Fordson, especially, a great amount of actual tractor field data was made available to designers. The Fordson more-or-less established the configuration of the "conventional" tractor. Many new tractors of the early twenties resembled the Fordson, at least externally. These included the McCormick-Deering 15-30 and 10-20, the General Motors Samson, and the John Deere Model D.

Despite its prominence, Farmall designers avoided being influenced by

Mary Lou Poch, New Holstein, Wisconsin, sits aboard her pride and joy: a 1936 Farmall F-12. Mary Lou is a secretary at Tecumseh Motors. She and husband John are working toward a collection of twenty-five classic tractors. Mary Lou's F-12 has the optional fenders, which cost the original owner about $12 extra.

the Fordson except in the areas of the lighter weight and lower cost. There were, however, several other designs and innovations that swayed all future tractor configurations—especially those of the Farmall.

The International Harvester Motor Cultivator

Between 1915 and 1918, Harvester's experimental engineers worked on a device for powered cultivation of such crops as corn and cotton. Ed Johnston and colleague C. W. Mott in 1916 filed for a patent for a specialized machine that "pushed" a two-row cultivator.

The device, called a "Motor Cultivator," had an unusual configuration. A four-cylinder engine rode directly above a pair of drive wheels positioned closely together and connected by a vertical driveshaft. This rear-drive element swiveled on the frame, around the driveshaft, for steering. The driver sat in front of the engine and had a steering wheel and levers for selecting forward and reverse. In front of the operator, cultivator shovels were mounted between a pair of non-steerable, wide-stance front wheels. About 300 Motor Cultivators were sold in 1917 and 1918, but the idea did not catch on and production ended in 1918.

Harvester learned several things from the Motor Cultivator: that good visibility was needed for cultivator work and that multiple-row cultivation worked. Experience with the rear-

Although its production was limited by the failure of its parent company, the Moline Universal was really the first all-purpose tractor. This example is on display in the Smithsonian Institution. Smithsonian Institution

wheel steering arrangement proved that it was not such a good idea. Rear-wheel steering is like a rudder on a boat: it swings the rear in the opposite direction from the desired course. On the Motor Cultivator, at least some of the shovels were mounted behind the front wheels. These shovels swung with the rear wheels toward the crops the farmer needed to avoid, rather than away from them, as steering corrections were made.

The Moline Universal

Introduced in 1917, the Moline Universal was an unusual contraption, even by the standards of those days. It was, however, the world's first successful all-purpose tractor.

The Universal's dominant feature was a pair of large drive wheels in the front, which provided the tractive effort and steering. Dolly wheels in the back were only used when no imple-

ment was installed; each implement had its own system for carrying the back end. The operator sat at the extreme rear, where he or she had a fairly good view of the implement ahead.

Other unique features of the Universal included adjustable drive wheel height, to keep the tractor level when one wheel was in a furrow; power lift; electric lights and starter; and an enclosed drivetrain and radiator.

The Universal was a success, but its parent company could not withstand the onslaught of the Fordson. The Universal was discontinued, and the

concept of the all-purpose tractor almost died as the Moline Plow Company struggled for its life.

Harvester's engineers adapted the longitudinal engine configuration and enclosed radiator, and learned the importance of engine air filtration—without an air filter, the life of the engine was short.

The Power Takeoff

One of International Harvester Company's initial responses to the competition of the Fordson was the development of the rear driveshaft-type power takeoff (PTO). In 1918, it came attached to a new small tractor, known as the 8-16. The 8-16 borrowed much of its configuration from the International truck line. The drive housing ended up with a 1.125in splined shaft sticking out. This was an idea from the fertile mind of Ed Johnston, who had seen a similar thing in France more than ten years earlier.

A French tractor experimenter by the name of Gougis was having trouble with a McCormick binder because of

John Poch's 1940 Farmall H on full steel. John has had the H for about nine years. It had been sold new on steel, but the original wheels had been cut off and converted to rubber. John had already purchased a full set of appropriate vintage steel wheels before he had the tractor. When he found the tractor, the engine was stuck but the sheet metal was good. To make the H more typical of the period, John removed the starter, lights, and generator.

10 speeds forward with TA

Torque Amplifier gives you *two* speeds in each gear. Extra, *in-between speeds* help you plant as fast as field conditions permit with accurate McCormick 2 and 4-row planters. You can change speed *on the go*, without shifting, to match planting speed to field conditions... slow for full-power turns in soft ground.

Plant on time... in shorter time
with FAST-HITCH, TORQUE AMPLIFIER and HYDRA-TOUCH...

McCormick® FARMALL® 300 and 400 tractors

Farm faster... make up weather delays... meet planting dates with a new work-speeding Farmall 300 or 400. Switch implements seconds-fast with Fast-Hitch to gain *extra* rounds.

Pull Torque Amplifier lever to increase pull-power up to 45% to eliminate down-shifting. Save time with Hydra-Touch—the most complete and convenient big implement control.

Hydra-Touch saves time on turns. "Live" 2-way hydraulic power raises or lowers 2 or 4-row Fast-Hitch planter fast! High lift keeps planter runners trash-free on turns. Hydra-Touch levers hold and return *automatically*—both hands are free for steering. When cultivating, you can control right, left and rear gangs *individually* or all together.

Fast-Hitch lets you switch in seconds from planting to disking—or bac again... to work up the seedbed just ahead of the planter and avoi costly redisking or harrowing in case of rains. Fast-Hitch "float" hel this McCormick mounted planter follow ground contour to drill (hill-drop at uniform depth.

Your IH dealer will gladly demonstrate Fast-Hitch, Torque Amplifier, Hydra-Touch and other farm-easy advantages like *completely* independent pto. See for yourself why Farmall 300 and 400 tractors lead in performance and value! Use the convenient IH Income Purchase Plan of Buying.

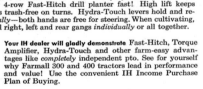

SEE YOUR
INTERNATIONAL
HARVESTER DEALER

International Harvester products pay for themselves in use—McCormick Farm Equipment and Farmall Tractors... Motor Trucks... Crawler and Utility Tractors and Power Units—General Office.

This 1956 Prairie Farmer ad touts the Fast Hitch and the Torque Amplifier. The Torque Amplifier, standard on the 300 and 400 models, provided a real competitive advantage over the rival John Deere 60 and 70. Note the short muffler used originally on both Farmall models.

wet, slippery ground. The bullwheel, which drove the binder mechanism, did not have sufficient traction, and in frustration, Gougis adapted a tumbling-rod drive between his tractor's engine and the binder, eliminating the bullwheel drive. Although crude, he saved his wheat harvest. Ed Johnston happened to be in International Har-

vester's Paris office when news of this event arrived. He visited Gougis, and did not forget what he saw.

To justify the splined extension shaft sticking out of the back of the 8-16, Johnston and his team immediately began inventing the PTO Binder. The binder was useful only if used with the 8-16. It's not clear whether the binder sold the 8-16, or vice versa. Nevertheless, considering the times, both were quite successful. PTOs were incorporated into the next Harvester tractors, and became standard equipment on the 10-20.

By 1922, it was recognized that an all-purpose tractor had to do more than just plow, cultivate, and provide belt power. To truly replace the horse, the tractor had to be able to apply its horsepower directly to implements such as this binder.

Available Implements

With the development of new PTO equipment came a new basis of designing a tractor's productivity output and configuration: the tools it had to work with. While the long-line implement makers offered equipment compatible with their tractors, farmers often did not use them, trying instead to modify horse-drawn implements. Not only was this less than satisfactory because of the difference in the horsepower applied, but another factor was now appearing: to be cost-effective, the tractor had to be laborsaving, as well. It was not feasible to have an implement operator as well as the tractor driver. What had to be developed were implements that could be controlled from the tractor seat, implements that would do the jobs of horse-drawn implements, but faster and better, and implements that would harness the tractor's power to do jobs the horse had not done.

For example, plows could be made to run deeper, improving the soil's fertility and tilth for alfalfa and similar crops. The tractor farmer soon found he or she was receiving real dividends.

The Farmall designers knew they had to envision new tools from the outset, thus developing beet pullers, corn binders and pickers, planters, spreaders, and haying equipment. Because the tractor's configuration was so different, many of these implements had to be custom-designed.

Evolution of the Configuration

After years of development and several prototype configurations, when the Farmall emerged in its final form it sold so well that the factory couldn't fill orders quickly enough and the Farmall soon engendered imitators. The conventional tractor configuration was eventually altered to be the Farmall type, rather than the standard-tread Fordson type.

The Farmall's two outstanding features were that it was tall and narrow. Actually, it was spindly, and looked like a milk stool or a three-legged spider. Its height enabled it to go over row crops such as corn, and its narrow front aided visibility. The tricycle front wheel arrangement allowed it to move between the rows and facilitated tight turns. Originally, the two wheels were set closely together vertically, but were later angled out at the top to prevent shimmy and to make steering easier.

Although the Farmall looked spindly, it was not as light as it looked. It was more than 1000lb heavier than a Fordson, and the weight was as far aft and as low as possible for good traction and stability.

With the proper implements, the Farmall "could perform all the farm tasks except milking," as Cyrus Hall McCormick III wrote in *The Century of the Reaper.* It could comfortably handle a two-bottom plow with 14in bottoms, it could drive a 22in thresher if the bundles weren't thrown in too quickly, it could cultivate four rows, it could drive PTO binders and mowers, and it could do other routine pulling and powering tasks around the farm.

Farmall Development

The Farmall was a far cry from the Motor Cultivator of 1918, but the heritage was obvious. Under the ominous clouds of Fordson market domination

in 1921, Ed Johnston was not given much time to marshal a defense. By then, the rear drive and pivoting engine of the Motor Cultivator had been changed. The engine was now fixed to the frame, with a drive arrangement to the front wheels. Steering was still at the back.

A late 1945 Farmall advertisement advocates the Farmall System, perhaps a veiled counter to the successful Ferguson System.

By 1920, the Motor Cultivator was unofficially known as the Farmall, and important changes had been made. The

The Farmall Regular is shown in this 1930 ad, which stresses that "Farmall" is an International Harvester name—an apparent attempt to thwart another brand's attempts to get in on the concept. Names such as "All-crop," "General Purpose," and "All-around" were proliferating; some unscrupulous salesmen were even referring to their row-crop tractors as "Farmalls."

transverse engine mounting had been changed to longitudinal, and the tractor was made reversible. For some applications, the driver sat facing the drive wheels; for others, the driver faced the close-set steering wheels. In this later direction, the machine began to take on the Farmall look. This is where Johnston found things when he called on Bert Benjamin to pull together, as rapidly as possible, an all-purpose Farmall.

Benjamin first eliminated the reversible seating with its vertical steering-wheel post. He substituted over-the-engine steering using a front wheel pivot and gearbox from an old IHC Mogul. He included detachable, front-mounted cultivator gangs.

By 1923, the configuration of the Farmall was fixed and a corporate naming committee officially gave the tractor the "Farmall" name and registered it as a trademark. Twenty-two copies of the 1923 version were made and sent to various places for testing—interestingly, places where the McCormick-Deering 10-20 was not selling well anyway, as management did not want farmers delaying purchases to wait for the Farmall.

Field engineers accompanied the tractors, and various implements—plows, harrows, planters, and cultivators—were tried. Later in the year, such items as crop dusters and mowers were added. Then came hillers, middle breakers, and PTO harvesters.

Also integral to the 1923 version was a unique cable-and-pulley affair that automatically applied one brake when the steering wheel was turned to its limit. Always a problem with tricycle tractors, the steering moment arm cannot be made as long as the designer would like without making the tractor too long. Bert Benjamin elected to use this mechanism, which came to be called the "triple control," and to keep the Farmall as short as possible.

Against the better judgment of many in Harvester marketing, the company decided on a production run of 200 Farmalls for 1924; the Marketing Department predicted that the new tractor would take sales away from the proven 10-20. Nevertheless, the price was set arbitrarily at a low $825, which was about the same as the 10-20 at that time.

Several improvements were made to the 1924 Farmall model. The rear axle housing was made heavier, as were the rear wheel hubs, transmission case, and drawbar. The frame was also strengthened and made from box-section steel, rather than channel steel.

The 1924 model used a tall air intake stack at the left side of the engine. A flannel cloth covered the intake in the first effort to get cleaner air for the engine. Beginning in 1925, an oil-bath air cleaner was mounted in front of the radiator.

For 1925, the price was raised to a more realistic $925. A total of 837 were built, with only minor changes in configuration from the 1924 model. To help placate the marketing staff and to avoid conflict with the McCormick-Deering 10-20, the Farmall did not receive a horsepower rating. In September 1925, however, the tractor was tested at the University of Nebraska (Test Number 117), so horsepower figures were soon well known.

Although the Farmall's engine displacement was 221ci versus 284ci for the 10-20, the power was almost the

The Farmall 300 was produced from 1954 to 1956. This 1956 model is owned by Austin Hurst of Lafayette, California.

same at 20hp. The reason for this was that the Farmall engine had a rated speed of 1200rpm, rather than the 1000rpm of the 10-20. Fuel for both was kerosene. As tested, the Farmall was almost 100lb heavier than the 10-20.

An experimental version of the Farmall from 1920.

The Nebraska Test report indicated that the 1925 version of the Farmall ran a total of thirty-nine hours during the rigorous testing, requiring neither repairs nor adjustments. It was an impressive debut for the world's first all-purpose row-crop tractor.

Full-Scale Production Begins

The Rock Island, Illinois, plant was ready to begin mass production of the Farmall in 1926. Alexander Legge purchased and then refurbished this structure, which ironically had been the former factory for the Moline Universal. It went on-line in time for 4,418 Farmalls to be completed that year. There was no longer any doubt about the acceptance of the all-purpose tractor. No longer was there any concern for hurting 10-20 sales. The problem

An experimental version of the Farmall from 1921.

now was producing enough Farmalls to meet demand.

The Farmall's configuration did not change much after 1925 until variations were introduced in 1931. A "Fairway" model—with special steel wheels customized for intended duties on golf courses and airports—was offered in addition to the regular Farmall.

By 1930, 200 Farmalls were being produced every day, for a grand total of 100,000 for that year. The team at International Harvester had beaten off the Fordson challenge and in the process changed farming just as surely as did the Fordson. While many horses were still providing farm power through World War II, the appearance of the Farmall spelled the end of horse farming. From 1926 on, it was more the result of an individual's economic situation that kept the horse in use; many farmers simply did not have the cash or credit to replace old Dobbin.

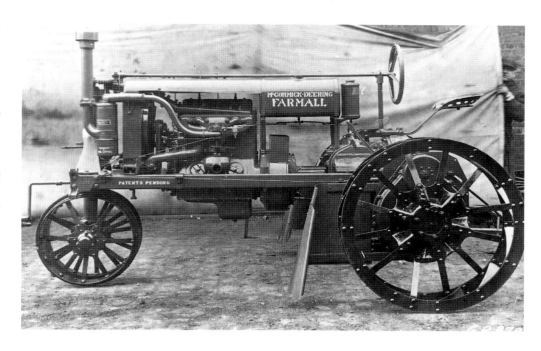

A "studio" photograph of the first production Farmall, 1924.

A Farmall 350 with a pull-type combine in tow. International Harvester power steering was an option on the 350. This Farmall is pictured at the Franklin Grove, Illinois, Living History Show in 1992.

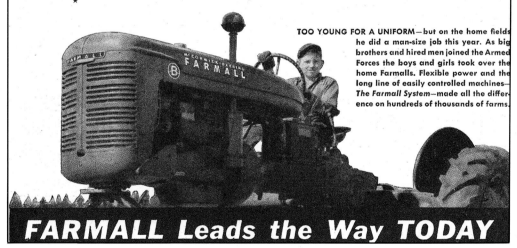

This wartime ad commemorates the twentieth Farmall birthday. The ad also commends youngsters for taking over farming duties when the men went to war. As the ad states, "Too young for a uniform—but on the home fields he did a man-size job this year."

A 1940 Farmall H on full steel, owned by John and Mary Lou Poch of New Holstein, Wisconsin. Although most of the H series tractors were sold on rubber, steel was an option until after World War II.

This 1934 Farmall F-20, owned by Steve Wade of Plainwell, Michigan, is equipped with an auxiliary road gear that gives a top speed of 18mph. This photograph was taken at the Prairieville Old-Fashioned Farms Days. Rubber tires were optional on the Farmall from 1933. The Farmall F-20 had adjustable rear wheel spacing. The wheels could be set at either 74in or 83in. Special narrow- and wide-front versions were also available: 57in or 77-in for the narrow, and 68in or 96in for the wide. Both versions were available with an adjustable wide-front axle.

A wide-front Farmall Model H, built in 1944. This is the same model and year tractor that the author drove as a 12-year-old lad in northern Wisconsin, working for a neighboring farmer. Such a striking piece of new machinery during the depths of the war years made a lasting impression on many. The tractor shown here, however, was photographed in the wet fields of Dorset, in photographer Andrew Morland's native England.

By 1956, when this 300 was new, there was not much call for belt pulleys; this live PTO, however, got a real workout. Owner Austin Hurst tells of mowing a great deal of acreage with a fast-hitch pitmanless mower—using fourth gear!

Chapter 4

Characteristics of the Farmall Models

F Series

Until 1936, all Farmalls were painted Battleship Gray. For the 1936 year model, the color Farmall Red was introduced. All the F Series, except some F-12s and F-14s (which were gasoline only), were started on gasoline and, after the manifold got hot, were operated on kerosene.

Farmall Regular

The McCormick-Deering Farmall, introduced in 1924, defined the row-crop tractor design. It was also the first of the all-purpose or general-purpose tractors, a concept that greatly broadened the usefulness of the farm tractor and affected the form of other configurations, as well.

Until the Farmall, farm tractors had gradually evolved from a modified steam traction engine into a foreshort-

This 1929 Farmall Regular is owned by Bill Rollinger of Pecatonica, Illinois. Son Jason is on the tractor, and son Billy rides the sickle-bar mower. Rollinger, a heavy construction equipment buyer, is an avid Farmall collector and an active participant in the Stephenson County Antique Engine Club Show in Freeport, Illinois. The Regular had a three-speed transmission and an all-gear final drive. Its four-cylinder engine produced 18hp at the belt in the University of Nebraska rated load test. Before other Farmall models were introduced in 1931, this tractor was simply known as the Farmall. When the others came out with F-number designations, it became conventional to refer to these earlier undesignated ones as Regulars.

ened highway truck arrangement. The rear wheels were larger than the front ones to carry the great weight over soft ground and to increase traction. Front wheels were smaller to facilitate a shorter turning radius without interfering with the frame and to cut costs. The front axle passed under the front of the tractor with kingpins on either end; crop clearance was thus dictated by the diameter of the front wheels. No attempt was made to raise the clearance, as no one except Farmall designer Bert Benjamin believed a full-sized tractor could be an effective cultivator.

Benjamin had experience with an experimental tractor configured to operate in either direction depending on the task assigned. This led him to the tricycle layout of the Farmall, with its two front wheels close together. The front wheels, being under the nose of the tractor, could pivot 90deg without interfering with the structure, and they could move between two crop rows, so as not to interfere with the taller crops. They dictated the height of the main body of the tractor.

To allow for reasonably sized rear wheels, drop gearing was used at the end of each rear drive axle. This caused the high torque to be developed as far down the geartrain as possible, reducing the loading on upstream gears and bearings.

Early in his experimenting with the tricycle configuration, Benjamin learned what anyone who has driven tricycle tractors knows: the steering

make a turn in minimum space, manually raise and lower the cultivator, adjust the throttle, and work the clutch. Automatic braking eased the workload at a critical time. The idea of putting both brake pedals on the right side near the right foot would not be implemented in the Farmall until 1939.

The new Farmall also featured a steering rod running over the top of the longitudinally installed four-cylinder, overhead-valve engine. The steering rod engaged a gearbox at the front, mounted on top of the steering post; this configuration became the norm for the industry, worldwide. The Farmall used a three-speed transmission, and also pioneered the use of implement mounting holes in the frame members on the forward part of the tractor.

The tractor was known as the McCormick-Deering Farmall until 1931 when the Model F-30 came out. After that, Farmalls built between 1924 and 1932—before its replacement, the F-20, was introduced—came to be known as the Farmall Regular.

A second version for industrial and golf course applications, the Fairway, was built until 1933. It featured special steel 40x16 rear wheels and 25x8 front wheels.

Farmall F-30

The first variation on Bert Benjamin's theme was the more powerful F-30. The Regular was considered a two-plow tractor, and the new F-30 was a three-plow model. It was designed for the larger farms in row-crop country where the big, standard-tread machines had already been in use. The idea was not so much to eliminate horses as to replace conventional competitive tractors. By 1931, there were a plethora of Farmall copies available from other manufacturers, so by introducing a second size of tractor, McCormick-Deering was turning up the competitive wick.

At 147in long, the new F-30 was 2ft longer than the Regular. It was also almost a ton heavier.

The engine for the F-30 was based on the successful engine in the 10-20

No attempt was made to muffle the exhaust of the Farmall Regular. Before 1931, there wasn't enough power to spare on muffling sound. Note the close proximity to the brass carburetor to help vaporize the kerosene. The Farmall series, except for the Cub, always used overhead-valve engines. Note also the removable port covers to facilitate bearing adjustment.

loses authority at high cramp angles. To overcome this, he incorporated an automatic, cable-actuated, individual rear wheel brake system. While this may seem overly complicated today, at the time it was not.

In 1924, many Farmall drivers had not previously driven a motor vehicle, let alone one with a four-row cultivator. At the end of the row, the farmer had to

A *Farmall Regular is put to the belt at the Midwest Thresherman's Reunion near Pontiac, Illinois. Note the cable along the frame rail which actuated the brake to assist the front wheels in steering.*

Production of the F-30 began in late 1931. It was the first variation on Bert R. Benjamin's theme, although the changes are hard to distinguish visually. The F-30 was longer and, at 5,300lb, much heavier than the 4000lb Regular. Production ended in 1939, but as with the F-20, tractors were completed from available parts and sold well into 1940. This example is owned by Bill Rollinger of Pecatonica, Illinois.

1. WHEN OPERATING ON DISTILLATE OR KEROSENE, DRAIN OIL TO LEVEL OF LOWER DRAIN COCK AFTER EVERY 10 HRS. OF RUNNING.
2. WHEN OPERATING ON GASOLINE DRAIN OIL TO LEVEL OF LOWER DRAIN COCK AFTER EVERY 30 HRS. OF RUNNING.
3. REFILL TO LEVEL OF TOP TEST COCK.
4. DRAIN CRANKCASE COMPLETELY EVERY 60 HRS. OF RUNNING AND REFILL TO LEVEL OF TOP TEST COCK.
5. OIL VALVE LEVERS DAILY.

Power for the Farmall F-20 came from a four-cylinder overhead-valve engine with a bore and stroke of 3.75x5.00in. Rated operating speed was 1200rpm. This power allowed the F-20 to pull two 14in bottoms. Thus equipped, the F-20 could plow about seven acres in a 10hr day on about 10gal of fuel.

conventional tractor. Otherwise, the F-30 kept the same configuration as the Regular. Remaining the same were the steering and brake arrangement, the engine placement and the three-speed transmission, thermo-syphon cooling, splash lubrication, and all-gear drive.

The McCormick-Deering W-30 was a standard-tread version of the Farmall F-30 introduced in 1932.

Previous page
The Farmall F-20. During 1932, the Regular was replaced by the F-20. Among the improvements was a four-speed transmission, instead of three; a 15 percent power increase through a half-inch increase in the bore; and a reduction in the belt pulley speed to bring belt speed to the new industry standard of 2395ft per minute. Farmalls were gray until 1936, when the color was changed to the now-familiar red. The Farmall's configuration is credited to International Harvester Engineer Bert R. Benjamin, whose efforts saved the company during the great tractor war of the twenties. This F-20 is owned by Steve Wade of Plainwell, Michigan.

A 1939 Farmall F-20 with owner Larry Gloyd aboard. This tractor was photographed on Independence Day at Gloyd's estate in the country outside Rockford, Illinois. Larry, who is CEO of CLARCOR, uses the tractor almost exclusively to give his grandchildren rides. He has owned the tractor for about four years.

By 1934, variations included a wide-front axle arrangement and conventional tread versions known as the W-30 and I-30. In 1936, pneumatic tires and electrical lighting became options. With factory rubber tires, a

high-speed fourth gear was installed. Late 1938 saw the availability of power lift.

Farmall F-20

During 1932, the Farmall Regular was updated and given the designation F-20. The engine cylinder bore was increased 0.50in to produce about 15 percent more power. To improve steering authority, length was increased from 123in to 140in. A four-speed transmission was added. The speed of the belt pulley was reduced from 690rpm to 650rpm to produce a belt speed close to the industry standard of 2395ft per

minute. The weight also increased because of these changes. The F-20 can generally be distinguished from the Regular by a shorter air intake stack.

Additional power made the F-20 capable of handling a 14in two-bottom plow. Thus equipped, it could plow about seven acres in a ten-hour day. The F-20 could handle a 22in threshing machine under most conditions.

The F-20 was available in regular and narrow versions, each of which had two optional rear wheel treads. The regular version rear wheels could be set at either 74in or 83in; the narrow version could be set at either 57in or 77in. By 1935, the narrow version could be ordered with a wide-front axle. In 1938, a wide version that could reach a 96in width was offered. An adjustable wide-front axle was available with that

version. A single-wheel front end was also an option instead of dual narrow wheels that year.

Production of the F-20 ended in 1939, although tractors were available from stock during part of 1940. Almost 150,000 were built, shattering all previous McCormick-Deering model production records.

Farmall F-12

Also introduced in 1932, the diminutive F-12 first appeared in late fall and only twenty-five were built that year. The F-12 was listed as a one-plow tractor, capable of pulling a 16in bottom. A PTO was included as standard equipment, as was, in 1934, fully adjustable rear wheel spacing.

The F-12 was originally equipped with a Waukesha engine, which was

The 1939 Farmall F-20 featured individual left and right foot-operated brakes, both on the right side of the platform. Production of the F-20 ended in 1939, although they were made from parts and sold into 1940. The F-20 was replaced on the International Harvester assembly line at Rock Island, Illinois, by the styled Farmall H. Almost 150,000 Farmall F-20s were built between 1932 and 1939, greatly exceeding the production volume of any previous International Harvester tractor. Although the F-20 was slightly longer and heavier than its predecessor, the Farmall Regular, there was really very little design change in Bert R. Benjamin's original concept between 1924 and 1939.

The Farmall F-12 featured a four-cylinder overhead-valve engine with a 3.00x4.00in bore and stroke. Displacement was 113ci, and rated operating speed was 1400rpm. The F-12 was available in either gasoline or kerosene versions. A McCormick carburetor was used. The diminutive F-12 was built between 1932 and 1938. Originally, it was available only in the single front wheel version, but soon dual-narrow-front, standard-tread, industrial, and orchard versions were also available. Note that there is very little camber angle on the front wheels. This is also the case with all the unstyled Farmalls.

soon replaced with one of Harvester's own, available in either gasoline or kerosene version. The early F-12s were equipped with a single front wheel.

Dual and wide fronts were offered later.

The F-12 could be adjusted to as narrow as 44.5in, approximately the width of a horse. This made it ideal for the truck gardener, who was used to one-horse specialized implements. With its standard PTO, the F-12 could handle a 10ft binder or a 6ft mounted mower. The 7ft turning radius of the F-12 allowed for neat mowing in a square pattern. Front-mounted equipment included cultivators, hay sweeps, and side-disk plows. The F-12 was available on factory rubber from its first full year of production.

Production of the F-12 ended in 1938. It was built in a standard-tread W-12 version, an I-12 industrial version, an O-12 orchard version, and a Fairway version for golf courses and airports.

Farmall F-14

Production of the F-12 ended in 1938 after more than 123,000 F-12s had been built. It was replaced by the almost-identical F-14. The only observable difference was that the engine was rated at 1650rpm, rather than 1400rpm. This change gave the F-14 about 14 percent more horsepower, enough to handle two 14in plow bottoms. It was available in either gasoline or kerosene burning versions and on either rubber or steel; wheel weights were optional equipment when rubber tires were used.

As with the F-12, there were standard-tread, Orchard, Fairway, and Industrial versions of the Farmall F-14. The serial numbering system for the F-14 began with 124000. A gap of several hundred numbers was left,

The right side of the Farmall F-12 engine showing the McCormick-built magneto. University of Nebraska Test Number 212, in 1933, indicated that the F-12 was capable of a maximum of 16.2 belt horsepower and 11.7 drawbar horsepower. It was capable of exerting a pull of more than 1800lb. Gasoline was the fuel used in Test Number 212. Similar results were recorded in Test Number 220 with kerosene fuel.

This 1939 Farmall F-14 with dual front wheels is owned by Bill Rollinger of Pecatonica, Illinois. The F-14 succeeded the F-12 in 1938. It was produced only in 19338 and 1939, with fewer than 30,000 being built. The F-14 was virtually identical to the F-12, except that the engine of the F-14 was rated at 1650rpm, rather than 1400rpm.

A 1939 Farmall A refurbished by Joe Schloskey, owner of Machinery Hill, a Phillips, Wisconsin, farm and industrial equipment dealer. Joe rebuilds one or two small tractors each year as fill-in work. He then adds a Woods mower deck and puts them on his sales lot. Thus equipped, these tractors are much in demand by those with above-average mowing requirements, especially anyone somewhat nostalgic for the finer old tractor.

Models A and C are featured in this 1952 Farmall advertisement.

rather than following the usual practice of beginning at serial number 501.

Despite vastly increasing competition, the F-14 sold well, with more than 27,000 units delivered in its two years of production. Competition in 1938 included the Henry Dreyfuss-styled John Deere Models A and B, direct competitors to the Farmalls. Minneapolis-Moline and Massey-Harris also introduced styled tractors. Allis-Chalmers came out with its Model B in 1938 and Model C in 1939.

Lettered Series

The real competition for all tractor makers came in June 1939 when a specter of the great tractor war of the twenties arose: Henry Ford was back in the tractor business. The late Elmer Baker, Jr., a staff writer for *Implement and Tractor* magazine, was quoted as saying, "Henry Ford had the time, money, and inclination to poke sticks at the McCormicks. He loved to, we've heard from the horse's mouth."

This time, the stick was the new Ford Model 9N tractor. This 2500lb tractor, selling for a mere $600, could plow more than 12 acres in a normal day, pulling two "fourteens"—better acreage than the expensive (more than $1,200) F-30 could do.

This unbelievable performance was made possible by the Ferguson implement system, the first volume-production application of the hydraulic three-point hitch. The system caused the weight of a variety of implements, plus their draft and suction loads, to bear down on the rear wheels, greatly improving traction.

The 9N was not a row-crop tractor in the true sense of the word, but its wide front did incorporate downward-extending kingpins that gave it fairly good crop clearance. Its cultivator was rear-mounted—and many a wise corn farmer would not take a chance to even try it.

According to extant reports, it worked quite well, however. The outcome is that Ford sold more than 10,000 9Ns in the six remaining months of 1939, despite the rush to production.

More than 220,000 Farmall A and Super A tractors were built between 1939 and 1954, attesting to their popularity. The Super A, introduced in 1947, was the same as the A, except hydraulic power was added for implement lifting. The Farmall A used essentially the same engine as the F-12 and F-14 Farmalls. It was available in both gasoline and kerosene versions. Rubber tires and a four-speed transmission were standard equipment. A higher crop-clearance Farmall AV version was available for cultivating such crops as asparagus. The A was considered a 16in one-bottom plow tractor. Most Super A tractors also had engines with a higher normal speed rating of 1650rpm, rather than the 1400rpm of the standard A.

The rush caused such severe production problems that the first 700, or so, 9Ns were shipped with cast-aluminum hoods, the steel stamping equipment not being ready in time. Almost 100,000 more of the little gray Ford-Fergusons were completed by the end of 1942, even with production curtailed by World War II. And just as the Farmall changed the configuration of the conventional tractor to that of the row-crop type, the Ford-Ferguson began to change it back to the wide-front type.

International Harvester was not caught napping by the competition this time. Seeing the trend toward more functional and eye-pleasing design, Harvester engaged the services of Raymond Loewy, a noted industrial designer who later gained worldwide renown with his rakish design of the Studebaker car line. Loewy was commissioned to overhaul the entire Harvester product line, from the company logo to product operator ergonomics.

By late 1938, the same year that John Deere introduced styled tractors, Harvester introduced the new TD-18 crawler tractor. The TD-18 was undeniably striking in its new, bright-red, smoothly contoured sheet metal hood and grille. Just months later, a new lineup of wheel tractors was announced, carrying the styling motif even farther with contoured fenders and styled wheels. The 1939 Loewy Farmalls still look stylish today.

Farmall A

The first and most radical of these new tractors was the Farmall A, which used the same engine as the F-12 and F-14 but governed at 1400rpm. Its most unusual feature was that the engine was offset to the left and the operator seat

Farmall B tractors were either dual or single wheel, narrow-front configurations, whereas the Farmall A was always a wide-front. Although the basic weight of the B was less than a ton, another ton of ballast could be added to provide traction and stability. The Farmall B was produced from 1939 to 1947.

Dan Langy maneuvers his 1941 Farmall B on his four-acre spread near Lena, Illinois. This 1941 Farmall B originally sold for a little under $650. The B was available in either kerosene or gasoline version. In Nebraska Test Number 331, the B developed a maximum belt horsepower of 16.8 and a maximum drawbar horsepower of 12.1. It also exerted a maximum pull of 2377lb, 64 percent of its weight. The Farmall B was essentially the same tractor as the A, but did not look like the A. The A had a long axle on the right side and a wide front. The Farmall B had two long axles and a narrow front. On the B, the engine was in the middle, rather than offset to the left as on the Farmall A. As shown here, however, the driver's seat is still offset to the right to provide an unobstructed view for cultivating.

and steering wheel were offset to the right. This gave the operator an unobstructed view of the ground beneath the tractor where the cultivator would be operating. Loewy called this concept "Culti-Vision." He reasoned that cultivating delicate crops was a major application of a tractor of this horsepower, and so shaped everything around this task.

Thus, the A was necessarily a wide-front machine to give the offset engine stability, but it retained the all-purpose functions for which Farmalls had become famous. It was equipped with both a belt pulley and a PTO, but the belt pulley was in the back, rather than at the side.

The new A was available with either gasoline or kerosene engines,

but as with all the Lettered Series tractors, gasoline predominated. The kerosene version used a compression ratio of 5:1, rather than the 6:1 of the gas engine. The thermo-syphon liquid cooling system was continued. This system operated on the gravity principle, rather than using a water pump; radiator shutters were used instead of a thermostat. Later versions of the A did use a pump-type system, however, and many have been converted over the years.

The A featured two wheel brake pedals on the right side of the platform that could be actuated individually or locked together. A Donaldson oil-bath air cleaner was standard equipment, as was a high-tension magneto with an impulse coupling. A Delco-Remy gen-

erator and electrical system were optional. The system included lights and
a starter. Rubber tires were standard,
as was a four-speed transmission with a
road gear giving a top speed of 10mph.

The Farmall AV was the identical
tractor, except it had longer front king-
pin extensions and 36x8 rear tires. This

arrangement provided an additional
6in of clearance for such crops as asparagus and sugar cane.

Farmall Super A

In 1947, a Super A version replaced the A. The Super A was identi-

*This 1941 Farmall B is owned by Mary Lou
and Dan Langy of Lena, Illinois. Except for
the wheel arrangement, the B was the same
tractor as the A. In fact, they were interspersed in the same serial numbering
system.*

cal to the A, except it had a built-in hydraulic system called "Touch Control," Harvester's first system for raising and lowering implements at the touch of a small lever. It consisted of three elements: an engine-driven gear pump, a double work cylinder, and a valve unit. Two rockshafts operated four rockshaft power arms to separately control left- and right-side implements.

Most Super A tractors had 1650rpm engines giving a substantial power boost. Production of the Super A continued through 1954.

Farmall B

The Farmall B was essentially the same tractor as the A—so much so, in fact, that the Bs were interspersed in the same serial numbering sequence. Model Bs do not look like Model As, though. The A has a long rear axle on the right and a short one on the left. The B has two long axles, one each on the left and right. Therefore, on the B, the engine is in the middle, rather than offset to the left as on the A. Nevertheless, the driver's seat is offset to the right and the steering column proceeds along the right side of the engine, as on the A.

All Model Bs were narrow-front, either single- or dual-wheel, and so followed in the tradition of the row-crop tractor. Rear wheels on both the A and B were reversible, to provide for row width changes of 28in. Both the A and B sold for about $600 in 1939, directly challenging the Ford-Ferguson 9N.

The basic B weighed about a ton, but adding a ballast could bring the weight up to almost two tons. Thus equipped, the B had little trouble with a 16in bottom pull-type plow. Other specialized implements included all of those for the A, except those requiring hydraulic power, as the B, unlike the Super A, was not made with internal hydraulics. Also, there were no Industrial or high-crop versions of the B.

Farmall C

The Farmall C more or less replaced the B in 1948. The same 113.1ci

This Farmall B is equipped with an after-market seat. Such seats, sold both as optional accessories and by other companies, greatly enhanced comfort and safety. Most farm equipment of this period used the simple, stamped steel pan seat. After ten hours of bouncing across plow furrows in such a seat, any farmer would welcome an improvement.

Instrumentation on the Farmall B was simple. The knob controlled the level of generator output. In the early forties, most tractors, including the Farmall B, used cutouts, rather than voltage regulators. Charging rate was upped when the lights were used.

engine was retained in either the gasoline or distillate configuration, as was the four-speed transmission. The big difference between the A and B Series and the C was that a steel rail frame was included in the C. The A and B did not have frames, but relied on the cast-iron

Unlike the Farmall A, the Farmall B had cultivator mounting pads at the front of the engine. The little B was unexcelled for row-crop cultivation. Rear wheel tread widths could be varied between 64in and 92in.

IH 5-STAR SERVICE begins for Roy Wishop when his IH dealer stops in to make an after-sale check-up on the new Super C and cultivator. "You and my boy Lowell sure see eye to eye on service," Roy tells his dealer, O. B. Lunde, of Worthington and Lunde, Rockford, Ill. "Why, if I'd let him, he'd be greasing and cleaning the Super C all day."

engine drivetrain for structure; the front ends were mounted to the front of the engine. The disadvantage of this arrangement was the lack of mounting places for front-mounted implements.

Along with the new frame, which was somewhat like that of the larger H and M models, came truly adjustable rear wheel spacing with sliding hubs. The A and B Series relied on reversible wheels.

The Model C was also fitted with hydraulic Touch Control.

Farmall Super C

The Super C replaced the C in 1951. The main feature of the Super C was an increase in engine displacement from 113.1ci to 122.7ci, through 0.125in increase in bore diameter. This gave the Super C a 15 percent increase in horsepower. The Super C was rated as a two 14in bottom plow tractor.

The Super C had other interesting new features. A new ball-ramp disc brake system allowed optional drive sprockets to be mounted outboard of the brake units to drive planters in direct proportion to travel. The seat was made more comfortable, with upholstering and an adjustable double-acting shock absorber and a conical coil spring. And, the hydraulic Touch Control system was standard, rather than optional.

The Super C was available in either dual tricycle or adjustable wide-front configuration. The C and the Super C can be readily distinguished from other tractors by their high steering-wheel position and the sharp angle the steering shaft makes as it proceeds past the left side of the cowling.

A Farmall C and a nice International pickup are shown in this ad which stresses 5-Star Service. The "See you at the polls" note at the bottom refers to the 1952 election in which Eisenhower was elected president.

Next page
The Farmall Super C replaced the C in 1951. Displacement in the Super C increased from 113ci to 123ci, giving it a much-needed power boost. The Super C could handle two 14in plows. Also new for the Super C were ball-ramp disc brakes.

The Farmall Cub was a unique approach to a utility tractor. It was the smallest in the International Harvester line, capable of pulling one 12in bottom. Introduced in 1947, the Cub was produced with little change until 1964. Variations, called International Cub Lo-boys, were continued for some time thereafter.

Mary Lou Langy's 1958 Farmall Cub. The Cub was the only Farmall with an L-head engine. It had a 60ci engine and a three-speed transmission.

Kathy Schultz of Deerfield, Wisconsin, poses with her 1957 Farmall Cub. The Cub is equipped with the unique one-armed front-end loader. Robert N. Pripps

Farmall Cub

For the tractor industry, 1947 was a watershed year. Enough time had transpired since the end of World War II for postwar designs to appear. The major companies knew they were in for a battle for market share, because there were just too many tractor makers competing. Furthermore, despite the war, the Ford-Ferguson was gaining momentum and sales at an exponential rate. International Harvester's response was to make improvements to its entire line and to introduce a new, smaller, less-expensive tractor, the Farmall Cub.

The Cub was aimed at the market the John Deere L and LA had been filling, meeting the needs of the vegetable grower, nursery, landscaper, and the small-acreage farmer still using only a team of draft animals. Interestingly, John Deere dropped out of this market in 1947 by replacing its small L and LA models with the Model M, designed to attack Ford head on.

The Cub was of the same configuration as the Farmall A, as cultivation of delicate plants was to be a priority job. Separately, it is difficult to tell an A from a Cub. Together, the Cub looks like a scale model. The most distinguishing visual feature of the Cub is the shape of the gas tank, which is rounded, rather than tear drop-shaped, as on the other Farmalls.

The 1500lb Cub used a unique little 59.5ci four-cylinder side-valve (L-

Next page
Owner Jon Kayser and the author's son, Greg Pripps, stand by Kayser's 1956 Farmall Cub Lo-Boy to show how low it really is. The Lo-Boy was designed primarily for mowing. The low stance gave it stability on the hills and the ability to slip under shrubs. Robert N. Pripps

head) engine, rather than the valve-in-head type used by the other Farmalls. This 10hp engine was also used in combines, pumps, blowers, and other implements. In the 1950 version, operating speed of the engine was raised from 1600rpm to 1800rpm, giving the Cub about 10 percent more power.

Seven or eight implements were custom built for the Cub, including a one-armed front-end loader. The tractor was equipped with magneto ignition, but an electrical system with

A 1948 Farmall Cub. The Cub was introduced in 1947 for the nurseries, vegetable growers, and the landscaper market. The Cub, like the Farmall A, was off-set to the left with the driver and steering wheel on the right. This concept was called "Culti Vision" by the Madison Avenue types, in reference to the great view the operator would have of a belly-mounted cultivator. The Cub used a unique 59.5ci side-valve engine operating at 1600rpm. This one is owned by Jon Kayser, a Case-IH dealer in Dell Rapids, South Dakota. Robert N. Pripps

starter and lights was also available. Other optional equipment included a rear PTO and hydraulic Touch Control system. The Cub, and its variations, continued in Harvester's inventory through 1964.

Farmall H

The Model H Farmall, introduced in 1939, replaced the F-20. Its main competitor was the John Deere B, which had been introduced in a styled version for 1938.

The engine developed for the H was a more modern high-speed unit of 152ci displacement, operating at a rated speed of 1650rpm. As such, it was in the 25hp class, the same as the older F-20. This power gave the H the capability to handle a 14in two-bottom plow or to drive a 22in thresher with relative ease.

The H was introduced at the same time as the big-brother M, sharing frame and layout, so that mounted implements were interchangeable.

Most Model Hs were equipped with gasoline engines, but distillate

Next page
A 1956 Lo-Boy Cub. Chrome hood insignias were used on later models, same as on the big tractors. Later Cubs were not Farmalls, but carried the "International" designation. The Cub Lo-Boy model had a height of only 63in as compared to the regular Cub, which stood 76in high. Otherwise, they were the same, using the same C-60 engine. Later Cubs, such as this 1956 model, had an rpm increase, which slightly raised the horsepower. Robert N. Pripps

The long and short of it. . . . John Kayser's Model HV high-crop and his Cub Lo-Boy stand side by side. The HV stands almost a yard taller. Robert N. Pripps

The Farmall H was a completely redesigned sequel to the Farmall F-20. The striking Loewy styling was both aesthetic and functional. Although it had about the same horsepower as the F-20, the H had a completely new engine that used a water pump, instead of the older thermosyphon system.

A fine example of classic tractor restoration, this 1942 Farmall H, serial number 97552, is owned by Leslie K. Bergquist of Maynard, Minnesota. Leslie did the restoration himself and says the tractor has "family ties."

This Farmall H was originally the basis of a cotton picker. Since converted to a standard Model H, it is now owned by Bill Rollinger of Pecatonica, Illinois. The only difference Bill can notice is in the configuration of the rear axle housings. Because of its infrequent usage, it still has the original S-3 Firestone tires.

versions were also available. Most were equipped with rubber tires, except those affected by the rubber shortages of World War II; during the war, many Model Hs were sold on steel wheels or with rubber fronts and steel rears. Most Model Hs were of the tricycle configuration, but wide-front, high-crop versions were also available. The Model H and the Model M used water-pump cooling systems; the earliest of these did not have pressure radiator caps.

Farmall Super H

In 1952, the Model H was upgraded to the Super H. The major difference was an increase in engine displacement to 164ci from the previous 152.1ci—boosting power to more than 30hp. This gave the Super H a true two-bottom (16in) or three-bottom

(14in) capacity. Basic weight increased about 700lb, but the Super H could be ballasted to around 8000lb.

The Super H was available in tricycle, adjustable wide-front or fixed wide-front high-crop versions. Hydraulics were optional. The Super H was equipped with the new International Harvester disc brakes, which used ball-ramp, self-energizing devices, in which the motion of the tractor tended to increase clamping forces on the discs.

Farmall M

The mighty M was the "big brother" to the H; they had the same frame and layout so that mounted implements could be interchangeable. It was the top of the Farmall line from

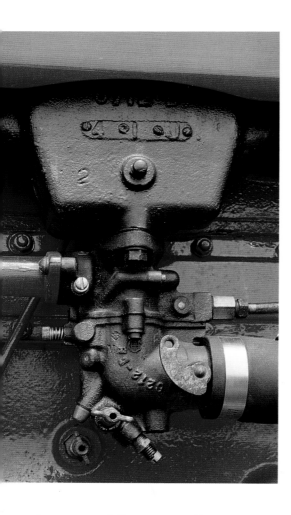

International Harvester made its own carburetors and governors. These are on a Farmall H. Most other tractor companies jobbed out components such as these. The H did use a Delco-Remy starter, a Rockford clutch, and a Donaldson air cleaner.

Farmall H serial number FBH377741 owned by Jon Kayser of Dell Rapids, South Dakota. The Farmall H was made virtually without change from 1939 to 1953. It was introduced as the successor to the F-20. The H used a 152ci engine operating at 1650rpm. It was rated for two 14in plows or a 22in thresher. Although most were of the dual tricycle configuration, wide-fronts (as shown here) and high-crop versions were also available. Jon's dad bought the tractor new in 1952. Someone bought it from Jon's dad and owned it for about six years before Jon bought it back. It still has the original tires on the back and its engine has never been overhauled. Robert N. Pripps

International Harvester made its own magnetos, this one on a Farmall H. It is of the high-tension type, with an auto impulse coupling.

The Farmall HV was a special high-clearance version of the famous Model H: note the high-arched front axle. The standard rear tires on the Farmall HV were actually smaller than on the regular Model H: 9.00x36 instead of 10.00x38. The difference was accommodated in the chain final drive, however, as the top speed of 15mph was the same for both versions. Jon Kayser's Farmall HV is serial number FBH-V 303312, making it a 1949 model. Robert N. Pripps

1939 to 1954, popular with large-acreage, row-crop farmers. Sales averaged more than 22,000 units per year.

The big 247.7ci engine, loafing along at only 1450rpm, produced enough power to easily handle three 16in bottoms. Fuel consumption was remarkably low; the M could be economically used for lighter chores, as well. Options included hydraulics, belt pulley, PTO, starter and lights, rubber tires, and a swinging drawbar.

The diesel MD was added to the line in 1941. The block part of the diesel engine was essentially the same as that of the gasoline engine. For diesel, aluminum pistons were used and the piston rings were thicker. A five-main bearing crankshaft was used, rather than the three-main bearing version of the gasoline engine. The head was, of course, completely different in that the compression ratio was more than dou-

bled to 14.2:1. It also contained the diesel starting system that allowed the engine to be started on gasoline and, when warm enough, switched over to diesel.

The engine was started on gasoline with the diesel governor control lever (throttle) closed and with the compression relief lever pulled. Pulling this lever did four things: the combustion chamber was enlarged, providing a compression ratio of 6.4:1; intake air was diverted through the starting carburetor; the ignition circuit was completed; and the carburetor float was released, allowing the carburetor to fill with fuel. After a minute of gasoline

operation, the compression relief lever
was pushed in and the diesel throttle
was opened, and operation switched to
diesel.

Although the MD cost half again
as much as a gasoline M, most farmers
found it well returned their invest-
ment. The MD used about one-third
less fuel than the frugal M. Those of us
old enough to remember the introduction of color television will also remember that diesel fuel was a little more
than half the price of gasoline in those

*The Farmall HV uses a special chain final
drive to raise the rear axle above tall crops
such as sugar cane, cotton, and corn. The
rear tread of this 1949 Farmall HV is
adjustable from 60in to 72in. The front is
adjustable from 60in to 66in by reversing
the wheels. This is somewhat limited as
compared to the standard Farmall H with
adjustable wide-front. Robert N. Pripps*

A 1953 Super H. Improvements over the Farmall H included a 164ci engine, a pressurized cooling system, and a deluxe hydraulic-snubber seat. Standard features included a swinging drawbar; an electrical system with generator, starter, and lights; a power takeoff and a belt pulley; and a hydraulic implement lift. Optional equipment offered included a hydraulic remote control, wheel weights, an hour meter, high-altitude pistons, magneto ignition, and fenders.

Dan Langy aboard a Farmall Super H owned by Frank Bunker of Milwaukee, Wisconsin. The Super H had a 29 percent power increase over the original H, making it a three-plow tractor.

days. The combination meant the price difference could be made up in about 1500 hours—about ten months for the average row-crop farmer in the forties.

The M could be ordered in high-crop, wide-front, or tricycle configuration.

Farmall Super M

In 1952, the Super M replaced the M. Engine displacement was upped to 263.9ci, giving the Super M a 22 percent power boost in the gasoline version and a 32 percent boost in the diesel version. It was also available with a liquefied petroleum gas (LPG) engine; during the fifties, this was a popular inexpensive fuel in many areas. It was also a cleaner fuel; no sludge or deposits were left in the engine, which meant about double engine life between overhauls.

The big news with the Super M was the MTA version, with the "TA" designation indicating "Torque Amplifier." The Torque Amplifier was a Harvester innovation in farm tractors, and the name became more-or-less generic as other brands picked up the idea. In operation, the Torque Amplifier provided a 1.482:1 ratio increase when actuated, resulting in an on-demand

Although considered a mid-sized tractor, the Farmall Super H could be ballasted to a total of 8000lb. The Super H was produced for fewer than two years; it replaced the Farmall H in 1953 and was replaced by the Farmall 300 in 1954.

Next page
"I've always enjoyed steel-wheeled farm tractors," says John Poch of New Holstein, Wisconsin. This 1940 Farmall M is in his collection of nineteen steel-wheeled tractors that he has acquired over the last eighteen years. His wife, Mary Lou, shares his enthusiasm.

Bill Rollinger's 1949 Farmall M, with Char-Lynn power steering. As with the Farmall H, the M could be obtained with either a distillate/kerosene engine or a high-compression gasoline engine.

power downshift to get through a tough spot without stopping to shift the main transmission down. It functioned much like "passing gear" in an automobile's automatic transmission.

The Torque Amplifier used a clutch-controlled planetary gearset that provided direct drive and an "underdrive" ratio for each of the transmis-

sion gears, effectively giving the Super MTA ten forward speeds and two in reverse. The MTA was the first Farmall with a live PTO.

Numbered Series

By 1954, the Korean War had ended. Eisenhower was president. Joe McCarthy was censored by the US

Senate. The economy was good, especially for the midwestern farmers who were finally making money in a peacetime economy.

Harry Ferguson had just won (after a fashion) his lawsuit against young Henry Ford for $340 million for loss of business and patent infringement. Ford had abrogated the Handshake Agreement his grandfather made with Ferguson in 1939, which had resulted in the Ford-Ferguson tractor. The outcome of the suit was that Ford paid Ferguson $9 million and agreed to stop using some of Ferguson's design ideas,

but the settlement did not include a prohibition against the use of the three-point hitch system. It was this system, which transformed the force required to pull an implement into weight on the rear wheels, that made the Ford-Ferguson the overwhelming sales leader for any size tractor. The fact that this system was not protected by the settlement meant it was up for grabs by all the other tractor makers.

The twelve major tractor makers had also become aware of a mood change in the row-crop farmer: these farmers wanted more power. The light-

The diesel option raised the price of the Farmall M from around $1,100 to just under $1,700. Most farmers who could afford the initial price found that the diesel paid off in fuel savings. The diesel provided 2.4 more horsepower hours per gallon of fuel than did the gasoline version. Also, diesel fuel cost only about two-thirds as much as gasoline in 1940.

duty use of cultivators on row-crop tractors for weed control was diminishing in favor of chemicals. Tractors were being used for higher-power applica-

The Farmall MD is such a capable and economical tractor that many are still at work on the farm. This 1946 example, owned by Aaron Woker, of Pearl City, Illinois, has been more-or-less put out to pasture, replaced by 806 and 1486 Internationals.

tions, such as multiple gang plows, followed by discs and drags, all hooked together. The first of the four-wheel-drive tractors since 1936, the Wagner, had been introduced, which boded the type of tractor of the future.

More power was the name of the game. Tractor dealers were selling high-altitude pistons for engines used at normal altitudes. Aftermarket turbochargers were installed and governors were set higher. The demand for more power was not only heard for the largest tractors, but across the entire line.

For International Harvester, things were happening too fast. In

Next page
Aaron Woker's 1946 Farmall MD. The block part of the diesel engine is the same as on the gasoline version, but the diesel used five main bearings, rather than three. Pistons and rings are also beefier. Farmalls, like other International Harvester diesel tractors, have dual combustion chambers. A compression relief lever opens a partition between them, lowering the compression and exposing spark plugs for starting on gasoline. Once running and warm, the partition is closed and the engine switches over to diesel operation.

96

Previous page
The 1946 Farmall MD owned by Aaron Woker of Pearl City, Illinois.

1953, John Deere introduced its Model 70, a top-end, row-crop tractor with more than 50hp. The Farmall Super M, brought out just the year before, offered only 44hp in the gasoline version. Besides, the Model 70, as well as the rest of the Deere line, could be equipped with "Power-Trol," Deere's

The Farmall Super M was noted for unexcelled lugging power. Engine torque peaked at about 360lb-ft at just under 1000rpm. The torque curve was essentially flat from there down to 750rpm (gasoline version). Combine that with the torque amplifier of the Super MTA, and there was not much that would bog it down. The standard rear tires of the Farmall Super M were 13-38s. For the fronts, 6.00x16s were used. The Super M (gasoline version) had a shipping weight of about 5600lb. With the optional wheel weights and calcium chloride liquid in the rear tires, the weight could be as high as 9000lb.

version of the weight-transferring three-point hitch. Harvester marketing knew that something had to be done for 1954 just to stay in the game.

Thus, the Numbered Series debuted in mid-1954, giving the impression that since the designations changed, this was a whole new lineup. Not much was done technically or cosmetically, but there was more power, at least in the larger Farmalls. Harvester managers could not, however, bring themselves to copy Harry Ferguson's three-point hitch. With dis-

Englishman John Friend is shown here plowing with his 1958 BMD, using a 1950s David Brown plow.

dain, they had treated it as a gimmick not needed by a real tractor, and now it seemed they were psychologically incapable of accepting it when it was handed to them as a gift. The fact that the three-point hitch was a real benefit to any size tractor, especially the smaller, lighter types, escaped them—and Harvester engineers came up with the "Fast Hitch."

The Fast Hitch was a two-point hitch that allowed for rapid coupling of hydraulically lifted mounted implements. It worked well enough, but it was, of course, incompatible with the three-point implements being standardized by other manufacturers and

such industry groups as the American Society of Agricultural Engineers. It wasn't until 1958 that International Harvester offered three-point hitches as an optional alternative to the Fast Hitch.

Farmall 100

The Farmall 100 was essentially the same as the Super A, except the engine displacement was increased from 113ci to 123ci and the compression ratio was increased from 6.0:1 to 6.5:1.

Next page
Manufactured in Doncaster, England, this Farmall BMD is pictured at the South Somerset Agricultural Preservation Club Show.

The rated speed was dropped from 1650rpm to 1400rpm. Although the Super A was not tested at Nebraska, it is estimated that these changes canceled each other out. Nevertheless, the 100 was rated for one 14in plow or two 12in plows.

Farmall 200

The Farmall 200 replaced the Super C. Both had a 123ci engine

101

Previous page
This 1958 British-built BMD has the optional adjustable wide front. Farmalls were also built in France and Germany.

operating at 1650rpm, but the compression ratio for the 200 was increased from 6.0:1 to 6.5:1, and therefore registered a little more horsepower in the Nebraska Tests. Other than changes to the grille and nameplates, the 200 was the same as the Super C.

Farmall 300

Real improvements in utility and productivity were incorporated into the 300. This tractor received the Fast Hitch implement lift, which made changing from one implement to an-

A 1958 Farmall Super BMD. This British-built version of the Super M is shown plowing in the wet September ground. At the wheel is John Friend of Pylle, Somerset. John uses the BMD regularly for plowing, baling, and rolling.

Previous page
The Super M had a 22 percent power increase over the Farmall M (gasoline version). The MD diesel version saw a 32 percent boost. The power increase was mainly due to a displacement increase to 264ci from 248ci. The Super M was also available in an LPG fuel version. Shown here is a 1952 Super M.

A Farmall 200, refurbished by Polacek Implement of Phillips, Wisconsin, sports a new Woods mower deck. Essentially the same as the Farmall C, the compression ratio of the 200 did increase from 6 to 6.5 to 1.

other faster and easier, and it had a live PTO and the Torque Amplifier. An increase in displacement and speed brought the 300's power up to more than 40hp. Otherwise, the 300 was essentially the same tractor as the Super H it replaced.

Farmall 400

As the replacement for the venerable M, the Farmall 400 was available

in either gasoline, LPG, or diesel model. A compression ratio increase on the non-diesel variants, plus breathing improvements, boosted power to more than 50hp for the first time—attaining parity with the John Deere 70. The Fast Hitch and Torque Amplifier were available, as was the live PTO.

Farmall Models After 1956

It was at about this point in the history of American agriculture—1963—that John Deere supplanted International Harvester as the largest

implement maker. Ford had persistently remained the supplier of the largest-selling single tractor model—more than 100,000 Ford 8Ns were sold in 1949—but as Ford diversified into multiple sizes after 1954, its total marketshare began to drop. The small, independent tractor makers all but disappeared—except for the makers of the four-wheel-drive monsters, such as Wagner and Steiger.

At Harvester, model numbers began to proliferate. The 100 and 200 became the 130 and 230, and the 300

In mid-1954, International Harvester introduced a whole new line of Farmalls. Shown here is a striking example of the result: the Model 300, basically replacing the H. Displacement on the Farmall 300 increased to 169ci from the 164ci of the Super H, through an increase in bore diameter of 1/16in. Rated engine speed was also increased to 2000rpm from 1650rpm, bringing the maximum belt horsepower up to 40, very close to that of the older Super M.

You don't have to be crazy to love old tractors, but some think it helps. Austin Hurst should know as he is a psychiatrist. His dad bought this Farmall 300 new in 1956, but sold it in 1969 when retiring from farming in northern Illinois. Austin bought it back in 1990. A friend of the family, John Bonjour, of Stockton, Illinois, overhauled it.

The Farmall 300 and 400 tractors were available in standard row-crop and high-clearance versions. Gasoline was the standard fuel, but the 400 was also available with a diesel or an LPG engine, and the 300 was also available with an LPG engine.

Next page
Most Farmalls of this era were delivered with dual narrow-front ends. The Farmall 300 was also available in a high-clearance and wide-front styles. With 40hp, the Farmall 300 was truly a three-plow tractor, but retained the maneuverability and utility of a mid-sized tractor.

A 1955 Farmall 300 with the optional wide-front front end. Owner William Kuhn bought this machine new. Now retired, he still uses the 300 on his small farm in Kinde, Michigan.

Air cleaner on an immaculately restored 1952 Super M.

and 400 became the 350 and 450. A big Model 600 was added in late 1956, but it was soon changed to 650. A white grille was added to all of these models. By 1958, a new sheet metal and grille suite were also added. The 130 and 230 became the 140 and 240, and the 350 and 450 became four models: 330, 340, 460, and 560. After that, the diversity of model numbers really took off.

By the late sixties, the numbers represented thoroughly modern and totally redesigned tractors. Big four-wheel-drive tractors were included in 1966; and in 1980, the Model 3788 was introduced. It was—and still is—one of the most advanced articulated four-wheel-drives made. It featured a "Control Center" cab aft of the articulation point and boasted four-wheel-drive traction with two-wheel-drive maneuverability.

The 1970s and 1980s were tough times for American implement makers.

Most, like Harvester, had not plowed enough profits back into plant upgrades and cost-reduction technology. Stockholder unrest caused many management changes as dividends fell. Bank interest rates went out the roof. Although the inflation rate, paralleling interest, made everything cost more tomorrow than today (which encouraged buying), money sources dried up and farmers were simply unable to borrow needed money for new equipment.

In the midst of all this, the United Auto Workers Union struck Harvester. The strike lasted only six months, but Harvester never recovered from it and the other financial woes of the times.

Finally, in 1988, Tenneco made Harvester management an offer for the Tractor and Implement Divisions that they could not refuse. Tenneco already had a foundering implement company, Harvester's arch-rival Case, but rea-

The Farmall 300 had all the modern conveniences: torque amplifier, live PTO, fast-hitch, and, best of all, a dipstick for checking the oil.

soned correctly that by combining the two, they could salvage the best of both worlds. Although it has made for some strange bedfellows, by this writing, some outstanding new tractor models have appeared. May the outstanding heritage of these two great companies fully combine to keep America and its farmers the food source for the world.

International Harvester initiated the numbered tractors to replace letter designations in mid-1954. Several improvements brought the tractors up to date. Fast-hitch was one improvement; the live PTO and Torque-Amplifier, available on some of the last of the lettered series, were now extended down the line. Power was increased; the Farmall 400 exceeded 50hp, a first for Farmall tractors.

Instrumentation and ergonomics were much improved on the numbered Farmalls that appeared in mid-1954. The lighted instrument panel contained oil pressure, ammeter, and coolant temperature gauges —and there was a cigarette lighter! On the numbered series Farmalls, introduced in 1954, the Torque Amplifier was available for both the 300 and 400 versions.

115

Previous page
A Farmall 350, the sequel to the 300 in late 1956. Displacement increased from 169ci to 175ci, and a "traction control" feature was added to the fast-hitch. The operator could now control the amount of implement-induced download on the rear wheels, making International Harvester's two-point hitch equivalent to the three-point hitch with draft control. The 350 could also be powered by a Continental diesel engine.

John Poch of New Holstein, Wisconsin, sits atop his 1958 Farmall 450. John is no stranger to equipment operation; he works as a forklift driver at Lake to Lake Dairy.

118

The Farmall 450 was built in 1957 and 1958 in diesel, gasoline, and LPG versions. It was considered a four-plow tractor.

Previous page
Nick Austin's McCormick Super BWD6 at the Great Dorset Steam Fair near Blandford, England. This tractor was purchased new by the Twizel Down horse racecourse at Fleet, Hampshire. It was sold to Nick in 1990 after thirty-five years of reliable service.

A British-built Farmall B450 diesel, photographed at the Great Dorset Steam Fair in Wincanton, England.

Nebraska Tractor Test

Early farmers were more often than not the victims of oversold, under-designed tractors. Dissemination of consumer information in those days was nothing like what we enjoy today. Unless someone in your neighborhood had a particular type of tractor, you were not likely to hear much about it. This was also true of other pieces of machinery and of automobiles, as well. Second, living in a rural area meant being isolated. Newspapers came by mail several days after the publishing date, radio was in its infancy, and publication of farming journals was just beginning. And finally, there were no standards by which mechanical things could be measured.

Because there were so many of them in those days, farmers had particular clout with the legislatures. They began to clamor for a national rating system for tractors, so that at least the power capability of a tractor could be understood. Competitive tractor trials in Winnipeg and other cities in the United States and Canada pointed out disparities between advertising claims and actual performance. These trials left much to be desired, as the tractors were often heavily modified by the factory and an army of mechanics and engineers kept them running long enough to compete. National legislation became bogged down in politics, however, and never came to pass.

A Nebraska farmer named Wilmot F. Crozier, who had also been a school teacher ("to support the farm," he said),

purchased a "Ford" tractor from the Minneapolis outfit not related to Henry Ford. The tractor was so unsatisfactory that he demanded that the company replace it. They did, but the replacement was worse. Crozier then bought a Bull tractor. This, too, was completely unsatisfactory. Next, he bought a 1918 Rumely "Three-plow." The Rumely met—even exceeded—Crozier's expectations; not only did it stand up to the strains of farming, but it could regularly pull a five-bottom plow. Shortly afterward, Crozier was elected to the Nebraska legislature.

In 1919, Representative Crozier and Senator Charles Warner introduced legislation that resulted in the "Nebraska Test Law." The law required

that any tractor sold in Nebraska had to be certified by the state. The state was to test the tractors to see that they lived up to their advertised claims. The tests were to be conducted by the University of Nebraska's Agricultural Engineering Department. L. W. Chase and Claude Shedd devised the tests and the test equipment, which have since become standards for the world.

The first test was made in the fall of 1919, of a Twin City 12-20, but could not be completed because of snowfall. The first completed test was made in the spring of 1920, and a certificate was issued for the Waterloo Boy Model N.

The results of tests of Farmalls between 1925 and 1957 follow.

Farmall Tests Summary

Model	Test Number	Fuel	Max. Horsepower Belt/PTO	Drawbar	Max. Pull	Fuel cons.	Weight	Wheels	Year
Regular	117	Kerosene	20.1	12.7	2727	9.39	4100	Steel	1925
F-30	198	Kerosene	32.8	24.6	4157	9.61	5990	Steel	1931
F-20	221	Kerosene	23.1	15.4	2334	10.4	4545	Steel	1934
F-20	264	Distillate	26.8	18.8	2799	9.82	4400	Steel	1936
F-20	276	Distillate	26.7	19.6	2927	10.5	4310	Steel	1936
F-12	212	Gas	16.2	10.1	1172	9.54	3280	Steel	1933
F-12	220	Kerosene	14.6	11.8	1814	10.0	3240	Steel	1933
F-14	297	Distillate	17.0	13.2	2369	10.9	4900	Rubber	1938
Cub	386	Gas	9.23	8.34	1596	10.9	1539	Rubber	1947
Cub	575	Gas	10.4	9.63	1605	9.38	2393	Rubber	1956
A	329	Gas	16.8	12.3	2387	12.0	3570	Rubber	1939
A	330	Distillate	16.5	15.2	2360	11.9	3500	Rubber	1939
B	331	Gas	16.8	12.1	2377	11.9	3740	Rubber	1939
B	332	Distillate	15.4	12.0	2463	11.8	3700	Rubber	1939
C	395	Gas	19.9	15.9	2902	11.2	4409	Rubber	1948
Super C	458	Gas	23.7	20.7	NA	10.8	5041	Rubber	1951

Farmall Tests Summary

Model	Test Number	Fuel	Max. Horsepower Belt/PTO	Drawbar	Max. Pull	Fuel cons.	Weight	Wheels	Year
H	333	Gas	24.3	19.8	3603	11.7	5550	Rubber	1939
H	334	Distillate	22.1	19.4	3169	11.8	5550	Rubber	1939
Super H	492	Gas	31.3	26.0	4178	11.7	6713	Rubber	1953
M	327	Distillate	34.2	25.5	4365	12.5	6770	Rubber	1939
M	328	Gas	36.1	24.5	4233	12.2	6770	Rubber	1939
MD	368	Distillate	35.0	NA	4541	14.6	7570	Rubber	1941
Super M	475	Gas	43.9	37.1	5676	12.0	8929	Rubber	1952
Super M	484	LPG	45.7	39.5	6115	8.76	9145	Rubber	1952
Super MD	477	Distillate	46.7	37.7	5772	13.9	9338	Rubber	1952

Model	Test Number	Fuel	Max. Horsepower Belt/PTO	Drawbar	Max. Pull	Fuel cons.	Weight	Wheels	Year
100	537	Gas	18.3	15.8	2503	10.6	4338	Rubber	1955
200	536	Gas	24.1	20.9	3166	10.8	5331	Rubber	1955
300	538	Gas	40.0	30.0	4852	11.8	8257	Rubber	1955
400	532	Gas	50.8	45.3	6508	12.1	9669	Rubber	1955
400	534	Distillate	46.7	41.6	6415	13.9	9700	Rubber	1955
400	571	LPG	52.4	46.7	6374	9.78	9900	Rubber	1956

Some Famous Farmall Competitors

Model	Test Number	Fuel	Max. Horsepower Belt/PTO	Drawbar	Max. Pull	Fuel cons.	Weight	Wheels	Year
Fordson	124	Kerosene	22.3	12.3	2142	8.95	3175	Steel	1926
Deere GP	153	Kerosene	25.0	17.2	2489	9.18	4265	Steel	1928
Deere A	335	Distillate	28.9	24.6	4110	11.3	6410	Rubber	1939
Ford 8N	443	Gas	25.5	20.8	2810	11.2	4043	Rubber	1950
AC WD45	563	Distillate	43.3	32.5	5908	14.0	9700	Rubber	1955

Notes on Nebraska Tractor Tests:

Belt/PTO Horsepower: This is Test C horsepower, the maximum attainable at the PTO or belt pulley. If the generator, hydraulic pump, etc., were not standard equipment, they were removed for these tests. Note that Nebraska test data published during this period are not corrected to standard atmospheric conditions.

Drawbar Horsepower: Taken from Test G data, it is based on maximum drawbar pull and speed. The difference between this and PTO horsepower is due to slippage and to the power required to move the tractor itself. The heavier the tractor, the less the slippage, but the more power required to move the tractor. Factory engineers looked for the ideal compromise.

Max. Pull: Test G. The pull, in pounds, used for calculating drawbar horsepower.

Fuel Cons.: The rate of fuel consumption in horsepower hours per gallon taken from Test C conditions. The higher the number, the better.

Weight: The weight of the tractor plus ballast in pounds. Ballast was often added for Test G and other heavy pulling tests and then was removed for other tests to improve performance.

Wheels: Steel or rubber.

Model, Serial Number, and Production Year Summary

This list provides a means of determining a tractor's model year by listing the beginning serial number for the production year.

Model	Beginning Serial Number	Year	
Regular &	QC501	1924	
Fairway	QC701	1925	
	QC1539	1926	
	T1569	1927	
	T15471	1928	
	T40370	1929	
	T75691	1930	
	T117784	1931	
	T131872	1932	
F-30	FB501	1931	
	FB1184	1932	
	FB4305	1933	
	FB5526	1934	
	FB7032	1935	
	FB10407	1936	
	FB18684	1937	
	FB27186	1938	
	FB29007	1939	
F-20	FA/TA501	1932	
	FA/TA3001	1933	
	TA135000	1934	To TA135661
	TA6382	1935	
	TA32716	1936	
	TA68749	1937	
	TA105597	1938	
	TA130865	1939	To TA134999
	TA135700	1939	
F-12	FS501	1932	
	FS526	1933	
	FS4881	1934	
	FS17411	1935	
	FS48660	1936	
	FS81837	1937	
	FS117518	1938	
F-14	FS124000	1938	
	FS139607	1939	

Model	Beginning Serial Number	Year
Cub	FCUB501	1947
	FCUB11348	1948
	FCUB57831	1949
	FCUB99536	1950
	FCUB121454	1951
	FCUB144455	1952
	FCUB162284	1953
	FCUB179412	1954
	FCUB186441	1955
	FCUB193658	1956
	FCUB198231	1957
A and B	501	1939
	6744	1940
	41500	1941
	80739	1942
	none	1943
	96390	1944
	113218	1945
	146700	1946
	1982964	1947
Super A	25001	1947
	250082	1948
	268196	1949
	281569	1950
	300126	1951
	324470	1952
	336880	1953
	353348	1954
C	FC501	1948
	FC22524	1949
	FC47010	1950
	FC71880	1951
Super C	FSC100001	1951
	FSC131157	1952
	FSC159130	1953
	FSC187788	1954

Prefix letters

A = FAA   B = FAB
AV = FAAV   BN = FABN
   Super A = SA

Model	Beginning Serial Number	Year
H	501	1939
	10653	1940
	52387	1941
	93237	1942
	12250	1943
	15051	1944
	186123	1945
	214820	1946
	241143	1947
	268991	1948
	300876	1949
	327975	1950
	351923	1951
	375861	1952
	390500	1953

Prefix Letters
H = FBH
HV = FBHV

Model	Beginning Serial Number	Year
Super H	501	1953
	22202	1954

Prefix Letters
F-SH, SHV

Model	Beginning Serial Number	Year
M	501	1939
	7240	1940
	25371	1941
	50988	1942
	60011	1943
	67424	1944
	88085	1945
	105564	1946
	122823	1947
	151708	1948
	180514	1949
	213579	1950
	247518	1951
	290923	1952

	Beginning Serial Number	**Year**		**Prefix Letters F-SM, M-TA**				F-300	501	1954
Prefix Letters									1779	1955
M = FBK	MD = FDBK			F-100	501	1954			23224	1956
MV = FBKV	MDV = FDBKV				1720	1955		F-400	501	1954
					12895	1956			2588	1955
Super M	501	1952		F-200	501	1954			29065	1956
	12516	1953			1032	1955				
	51977	1954			10904	1956				

Farmall Tractor Specifications

Model	Year	Bore/Stroke (in)	Disp. (ci)	Comp. Ratio	Rated rpm	Forward Speeds	Basic Weight (lb)	Rear Tire Size (in)
Regular	1924-1932	3.75x5.00	220.9	4.5:1	1200	3	4100	40x6
F-30	1931-1939	4.25x5.00	283.7	4.5:1	1150	3	5990	42x12
F-20	1932-1939	3.75x5.00	220.9	4.5:1	1200	4	4545	40x6
F-12	1932-1938	3.00x4.00	113.1	4.5:1	1400	3	3280	54x6
F-14	1938-1939	3.00x4.00	113.1	4.5:1	1650	3	3820	
Cub	1947-1955	2.62x2.75	59.5	6.5:1	1600	3	1540	8x24
A	1939-1947	3.00x4.00	113.1	6.0:1	1400	4	2014	8x24
B	1939-1951				1400		2150	9x24
Super A	1947-1954				1650		2363	
C	1948-1951	3.00x4.00	113.1	6.0:1	1650	4	2845	9x36
Super C	1951-1954	3.13x4.00	122.7	6.0:1	1650	4	3209	10x36
H	1939-1952	3.38x4.25	152.1	5.9:1	1650	5	3694	10x36
Super H	1952-1954	3.50x4.25	164.0	6.0:1	1650	5	4389	11x38
M	1939-1952	3.88x5.25	247.7	5.7:1	1450	5	4858	11x38
MD	1941-1951	3.88x5.25	247.7	14.2	1450	5	5300	12x38
Super M	1952-1954	4.00x5.25	263.9	5.9:1	1450	5	5600	13x38
Super MD				16.5	1450		6034	
100	1954-1956	3.13x4.00	122.7	6.5:1	1400	4	3038	11x24
200	1954-1956	3.13x4.00	122.7	6.5:1	1650	4	3541	10x36
300	1954-1956	3.56x4.25	169.2	6.3:1	1750	5	4800	11x38
400	1954-1956	4.00x5.25	263.9	G 6.3 D16.5	1450	5	6519	11x38

Clubs and Newsletters

Books

The following books offered essential background on the International Harvester Company's origins and history, and about the tractors and equipment of the times. These make good reading and library additions for any Farmall buff. Most are available from Motorbooks International Publishers & Wholesalers, PO Box 2, 729 Prospect Avenue, Osceola, Wisconsin 54020 USA, or by calling 800-826-6600.

The Agricultural Tractor 1855–1950 by R. B. Gray. Society of Agricultural Engineers. An outstanding and complete photo history of the origin and development of the tractor.

The American Farm Tractor by Randy Leffingwell. Motorbooks International. A full-color hardback history of all the great American tractor makes.

The Century of the Reaper by Cyrus McCormick. Houghton Mifflin Company. A first-hand account of the Harvester and Tractor Wars by the grandson of the inventor.

A Corporate Tragedy by Barbara Marsh. Doubleday and Company. An intriguing account of the development of International Harvester Company and its ultimate sale of the farm equipment business to Tenneco in 1988. Much scholarly research and journalistic writing are evinced in this work; a "must read" for Farmall fans.

The Development of American Agriculture by Willard W. Cochrane. University of Minnesota Press. An analytical history.

Farm Tractors 1926–1956 edited by Randy Stephens. Intertec Publishing. A compilation of pages from *The Cooperative Tractor Catalog* and the *Red Tractor Book.*

Fordson, Farmall and Poppin' Johnny by Robert C. Williams. University of Illinois Press. A history of the farm tractor and its impact on America.

Ford Tractors by Robert N. Pripps and Andrew Morland. Motorbooks International. A full-color history of the Fordson, Ford-Ferguson, Ferguson, and Ford tractors, covering the influence of these historic tractors on tractor design.

Ford and Fordson Tractors by Michael Williams. Blandford Press. A history of Henry Ford and his tractors, especially concentrating on the Fordson.

Harvest Triumphant by Merrill Denison. William Collins Sons & Company Ltd. The story of human achievement in the development of agricultural tools, especially that in Canada, and the rise to prominence of Massey Harris Ferguson (now known as the Verity Corporation). Rich in the romance of farm life in the last century and covering the early days of the Industrial Revolution.

How to Restore Your Farm Tractor by Robert N. Pripps. Motorbooks International. Follows two tractors through professional restoration, one a 1939 Farmall A. Includes tips and techniques, commentary, and photos.

International Harvester Tractors by Henry Rasmussen. Motorbooks International. A photo essay on "Reliable Red."

Threshers by Robert N. Pripps and Andrew Morland. Motorbooks International. A full-color history of grain harvesting and threshing, featuring photos and descriptions of many of the big threshers in operation.

The Yearbook of Agriculture—1960. U.S. Department of Agriculture.

150 Years of International Harvester by C. H. Wendel. Crestline Publishing. A complete photo-documented product history of International Harvester.

Stemgas Publishing Company issues an annual directory of engine and threshing shows. Its address is: P.O. Box 328, Lancaster, Pennsylvania 17603; 717-392-0733. The cost of the directory has been $5.00. Stemgas also publishes *Gas Engine Magazine* and *Iron-men Album,* magazines for the enthusiast.

Clubs and Newsletters

Newsletters providing a wealth of information and lore about individual brands of antique farm tractors and equipment have been on the scene for some time. More are being published each year, so the following list is far from complete.

Antique Power
Patrick Ertel, editor
PO Box 838
Yellow Springs, OH 45387

Green Magazine (John Deere)
R. & C. Hain, editors
RR 1
Bee, NE 68314

M-M Corresponder (Minneapolis-Moline)
Roger Mohr, editor
Rt 1, Box 153
Vail, IA 51465

9N-2N-8N Newsletter (Ford)
G. W. Rinaldi, editor
154 Blackwood Lane
Stamford, CT 06903

Old Abe's News (Case)
David T. Erb, editor
Rt 2, Box 2427
Vinton, OH 45686

Old Allis News (Allis Chalmers)
Nan Jones, editor
10925 Love Road
Belleview, MI 49021

Oliver Collector's News
Dennis Gerszewski, editor
Rt 1
Manvel, ND 58256

Prairie Gold Rush (Minneapolis-Moline)
R. Baumgartner, editor
Rt 1
Walnut, IL 61376

Red Power (International Harvester)
Daryl Miller, editor
Box 277
Battle Creek, IA 51006

Wild Harvest (Massey-Harris, Ferguson)
Keith Oltrogge, editor
1010 S Powell, Box 529
Denver, IA 50622

Index